GULZAR'S
Ijaazat

INSIGHTS INTO THE FILM

MIRA HASHMI

HarperCollins *Publishers* India

First published in India by
HarperCollins *Publishers* in 2019
A-75, Sector 57, Noida, Uttar Pradesh 201301, India
www.harpercollins.co.in

2 4 6 8 10 9 7 5 3 1

P-ISBN: 978-93-5302-510-6
E-ISBN: 978-93-5302-511-3

Typeset in 11.5/15 Bembo at
Manipal Digital Systems, Manipal

Printed and bound at
Thomson Press (India) Ltd

For Shoaib 'Puppi' Hashmi and Salima 'Cheemie' Hashmi,
my parents, my champions

Contents

CR

CONTENTS

Preface

∞

Although Hindi films had been banned in Pakistani cinemas for over forty years (1965–2007), Hindi film fans in the country found an oasis in the late 1970s in the form of the pirated VHS tapes that found their way into Pakistani households through expatriate communities living in the UAE and Hong Kong. Filmi publications like *Stardust*, *Filmfare* and the now-defunct *Star & Style* too, were smuggled into local bookshops through increasingly imaginative means. Our local TV antennae caught whiffs of Doordarshan, and *Chitrahaar* became a staple twice-weekly indulgence, with Vicco Turmeric Ayurvedic Cream and Nirma Washing Powder ads sounding the clarion call to come and partake.

As a result, I grew up on a robust diet of Hindi films. I didn't just develop a taste for the masala; I became an addict. I also, at some point, became acutely aware that though virtually all of these films were in some way or the other, directly or indirectly, about romance, very few of them were about relationships. Love and/or marriage always seemed to be an end-goal, never a journey. Love was the impetus to fight against villains – whether they were smirking smugglers, evil dacoits, unsympathetic parents, economic disparities or just society at large – and marriage was the ultimate reward. There was the odd 'sad ending', of course, where one or both of the lovers would give up their life in order to be united in death rather than be separated while alive; but even here, the romantic union was presented as the be-all and end-all of existence. The overwhelming majority of films, however, ended with the final shot of happily-ever-after smiles and embraces, as a romantic duet from an earlier part of the film played in the background and the 'The End' was superimposed on the screen as a declaration that the story had reached its conclusion and nothing further remained to be said. As I grew into teendom, I found that my actual interest in the story began where the film usually chose to end it. Instead of providing satisfaction and closure, 'The End' only served to frustrate me in the same way that childhood fairytales had before. 'So, Cinderella and the prince got hitched,' I'd think to myself. 'Now what? They hardly know each other. Will they be compatible? What if he leaves her alone all the time to go off hunting with his debauched friends and she becomes an alcoholic, wasting away in that huge palace?'

Similarly, I wondered what the future had in store for the other film couples; what would happen once the love goggles reached their expiration date, as they inevitably do in real life, and the warts revealed themselves? Would love still be able to conquer in the face of the monotony of domestic life, personality clashes, goals and dreams evolving in separate directions, and such practicalities, or would it give up and walk away in search of greener, less demanding pastures? (Perhaps this was one of the reasons why Ramesh Talwar's 1977 film *Doosra Aadmi* stood out for me; it was one of the rare commercial films that examined the thorns, rather than the bed of roses, in a marriage.)

Somewhere in the midst of this, as if by divine machination, I discovered the cinema of Gulzar. I'm talking about the late 1980s here so you may well be rightly wondering, 'But he had been making films since the early '70s; were you living under a rock?' Of sorts, yes. You see, those precious VHS copies of Hindi films that most local rental places stocked in the initial years of the decade were usually the latest Amitabh-Mithun-Sridevi-Jeetendra potboilers; very few imagined that their customers would be interested in older films, least of all old *arty* films. But as the video rental business boomed and the audience for it grew, so expanded the audience's taste and, with it, the demand for a wider variety of cinematic fare – particularly the classics. The video hunter–gatherers obliged and rental stores started stocking fairly diverse titles, from the celebrated to the relatively obscure. And so it came to be that most of the then–younger generation saw *Mughal-e-Azam* (1960), *Awaara* (1951), *Sholay* (1975), etc., well after we had seen the likes of *Himmatwala* (1998), *Disco Dancer* (1982) and *Shahenshah* (1988). (And, yes, probably just as many Pakistanis have tried to freeze-frame Mandakini under the waterfall in *Ram Teri Ganga Maili* [1985] as Indians.)

Of course, we had been watching and listening to songs from Gulzar's films on *Chitrahaar* and on smuggled audio cassettes for years; we even knew the dialogue prelude to '*Tere bina zindagi se koi shikva to nahi*' from *Aandhi* (1975) by heart. But, finally, we were able to put those songs in context. As it happened, *Aandhi* was the first one to be viewed in my household, accompanied by whispers of it being a fictionalized account of Indira Gandhi's private life. Many were astounded by its open ending, which not only daringly defied Hindi cinema's penchant for upholding the notion of 'love conquers all', but also suggested that for some women – shock, horror! – life possibly had meaning beyond romance and matrimony. I was intrigued and sought out more of the writer-director's work, which in the pre-Internet days, with almost non–existent access to published information about the Hindi film history, was not an easy task. I don't quite recall how I managed it; the most important part is that I did, so I begged and bullied my video-*wala* into procuring for me several of Gulzar's directorial efforts, like *Koshish* (1972), *Parichay* (1972), *Mausam* (1975), *Khushboo* (1975), *Kinara* (1977) and *Angoor* (1982), as well as some of the films he had had a hand in writing, like *Anand* (1971), *Chupke Chupke* (1975), *Khubsoorat* (1980) and other popular 'middle-of-the-road' films (as they were often called) directed by Hrishikesh Mukherjee. Needless to say, it soon dawned upon me that not only had Gulzar been on writing and directing duties for some remarkable films, he was also responsible for some of the most memorable and modern lyrics ever heard in Hindi film songs. Most importantly, though, his films delved into the very fabric of human interaction and relationships, looking deeply into what made the fibres tear and what, sometimes, could stitch them back together, even momentarily. Love, his stories seemed to say, is not always the answer; rather, it is just a part of the question.

Biographer Saibal Chatterjee writes in the introduction to *Echoes & Eloquences: The Life and Cinema of Gulzar*:

Gulzar's significance as a filmmaker stems from the singularity of his vision. In a movie industry that is propelled largely by the desire for making a box-office killing, he dares to make films for the love of making them. He tells stories because he has tangible insights to share with his audience. He writes lyrics because he is a poet forever keen to give free rein to his imagination. Moreover, in an industry that does not encourage filmmakers to express their inner feelings and ideas – popular Hindi cinema is a vehicle of formulaic, simplistic stories of love and heroism, good and evil, sacrifice and avarice – he dares to use his tools to articulate his humanist vision and his inner self. [1]

Gulzar himself has stated, 'My films, I would say, are about human relationships. Other things happen in my stories as well, but my camera remains focused on the human angle. [They] have always projected unrest, whether individual or societal.'[2]

Where *Parichay* charmed with its modest and subtle take on *The Sound of Music* (1965), *Koshish* moved with its complex yet accessible exploration of the kind of lives either left unexamined by the mainstream Hindi cinema or only used cynically to milk a bit of pathos now and then. One could scarcely believe that the same pen and baton put forth the sophisticated yet screamingly funny comedy of *Angoor*, wherein Sanjeev Kumar, Deven Verma and the woefully underrated Moushumi Chatterjee raised the bar

1   Saibal Chatterjee, *Echoes & Eloquences: The Life and Cinema of Gulzar*, New Delhi: Rupa & Co, 2007, p. 5.

2   Bhawana Somaaya, *Talking Cinema: Conversations with Actors and Film-Makers*, Noida: Harper Collins Publishers India, 2013, p. 125.

for comedic performances to an enviable high. Here was a filmmaker and writer who knew how to translate word to image and was more than adept at coaxing the absolute best out of his actors.

No wonder, then, that a number of film stars turned to Gulzar when the urge to test the limits of their craft came upon them. Sanjeev Kumar, one of the actors who continually and successfully negotiated his way around the art–commerce divide in Hindi cinema, famously became Gulzar's muse and a regular player in his work. Perhaps the most conspicuous jump from masala to middle-of-the-road was that of Jeetendra, the most 'commercial' of actors if ever there was one. He both acted in and produced *Parichay* and went on to star in two more Gulzar productions, *Khushboo* and *Kinara*, in which he was joined by the most commercially successful actress of that day: superstar Hema Malini. Like *Aandhi*, the latter two films revisited, albeit in very different ways, what seemed to be becoming a recurring theme for Gulzar: a failed relationship afforded a second chance by a strange, often innocuous, twist of fate. *Khushboo*, for me, is possibly the most haunting, with R.D. Burman's achingly beautiful song score providing a befitting mellifluous backdrop. Burman and Gulzar together, of course, formed what was possibly Hindi cinema's most enduring and artistically revered composing-songwriting duo.

Ijaazat (1987), which came ten years after *Kinara*, can certainly be watched as a companion piece to these three films. A quadrology, if you will. Like the previous films, *Ijaazat*, too, was a story about a relationship revisited and re-examined, wherein the characters invite the audience to imagine a different denouement for the couple the second time life brings them together. Cinematically, *Ijaazat* may be more modest than some of Gulzar's other works, but thematically it was possibly his most daring film and one whose popularity among fans has only grown with time. Love triangles had been done to death in both Western and Indian cinema; only Gulzar could be expected to bring an entirely fresh, startlingly mature take to the hackneyed subject. It was an interpretation that was years ahead of its time, and merits a closer look.

Unless otherwise noted, Gulzar saheb's recollections about the making of *Ijaazat* in this book are based on an interview I conducted with him in Mumbai over two days in July 2015. The same is the case with the thoughts and memories recounted by Naseeruddin Shah and Anuradha Patel. Rekhaji did not consent to our conversation being recorded – 'People have misused my voice in the past' – but set me a challenge to take notes by hand as we talked. I have tried to reproduce her words as accurately as possible.

chapter one

Mere Nangay Pairon Mein Zameen Hai

In the Beginning

ॐ

'We must be grateful to Indian cinema because films gave the poet a livelihood and a position of prominence. I am sure no one would have offered me a thousand-rupee job outside of films.'

– Gulzar[3]

In the time before the advent of the Internet, particularly social media, the topic of Gulzar's real birth name certainly must have made for a great movie trivia question or a fact that could be brought up as a party piece to show off one's credentials as a true Hindi cinema fan. Of course, now,

---

3 Gulzar and Nasreen M. Kabir, *In the Company of a Poet*, New Delhi: Rainlight, 2012, p. 32.

thanks to the ubiquity of Wiki-style sites, it's no longer the revelation that it once was to learn that the name in question is Sampooran Singh Kalra, a moniker long ago relegated to official documents – like passport or tax forms – in favour of the celebrated nom de plume that the writer-poet-filmmaker chose for himself over sixty years ago when he first started writing professionally. 'It is traditional for a poet to have a *takhallus*, a pen name,' he has said. '[It] makes you feel important.'[4] Born in Jhelum district, West Punjab, in 1934, but brought up in Delhi after Partition, Gulzar was greatly influenced by UP's cultural and linguistic traditions that permeated the capital city's society at the time. It was this influence that he cited as the reason for his distinctly classical Urdu *lehja* (diction) and his love for the language itself, as well as its rich literary heritage. Bengali culture has had a similarly profound impact on his life and work, springing, in part, from his fascination with Rabindranath Tagore as both a writer and a personality. A fluent Bengali speaker, Gulzar recounted amusedly that he had often been mistaken for a true-blue Bengali. What a long and winding, and strangely apt trajectory for a man born to a Punjabi-speaking Sikh household in the heart of the plains!

While Gulzar's paternal grandfather, Nihal Singh, had been a cowherd and *gwala* (milk-seller), his father, Sardar Makhan Singh Kalra, having studied till fourth standard

---

4   Ibid., p. 13.

(which was considered quite an academic achievement for a boy of such modest means), had different ambitions. After his first job as a cook, he eventually established a fairly successful business selling cloth, initially in his native town of Dina and then also in Delhi, where he opened a fabric shop in Sadar Bazaar. It should come as no surprise, then, that Gulzar's daughter Meghna's famous pet name, Bosky, is actually the name of a cream-coloured Chinese silk once greatly favoured by aristocrats. Gulzar also once (only half-jokingly) told famed producer J. Om Prakash that if he were to ever have a son, he'd name him 'Lattha' – the name of another fabric.

It was due to the burgeoning success of his business in Delhi that the senior Kalra was compelled to move to the faraway city, even as the rest of his family stayed behind in Dina. But young Sampooran Singh, very much attached to his father, could not bear the thought of separation and wept inconsolably while seeing him off at the railway station. The father was moved by his son's display of emotion and decided to have him come live in Delhi. It was here, at age seven, that Gulzar saw his first film in a cinema – Sohrab Modi's *Sikandar* (1941), with Prithviraj Kapoor playing Alexander the Great. Little did the boy know, that in the coming decades, he would forge important and indelible associations with many succeeding generations of the actor's family. *Sikandar* left a tremendous impression on him, as did other films that he was allowed to watch by his father; this in itself was a boon since moviegoing was quite a taboo at the time, particularly for children. Another film he saw as a child that would later link up with his professional life was Mehboob Khan's *Najma* (1943); its leading lady, Veena, whose dimpled smile reminded Gulzar of his sister Mahinder, was cast as a landowner in the film *Aashirwad*, a film he wrote for Hrishikesh Mukherjee in 1968.

The cataclysmic events of the Partition disrupted the pleasant but mundane life at the Kalra household as refugees poured into the city, including relatives from across the border seeking accommodation and assistance. Makhan Singh had a large family as it was (Gulzar was one of nine children) and he had to think on his feet to deal with the burden of the added responsibilities he was compelled to take on. The brood thus ended up being divided into separate groups and sent off to live in different cities. Some of Gulzar's elder siblings had already established themselves elsewhere, most significantly his brother Jasmer who was settled in Bombay and ran a steady petrochemicals business.

Two years later, it was decided that fifteen-year-old Sampooran Singh should leave Delhi and join Jasmer Singh in Bombay instead, the prevalent wisdom being that the metropolis would provide bigger and better opportunities to the scion of a 'business' family. They could not have known that the young man's interests lay well away from both cloth and petrol.

So it was that Gulzar came to live with his elder brother, joined Khalsa College as a student and worked after college hours at Jasmer's petrol pump. Meanwhile, while he may have come to the city of celluloid dreams, it was for literature and writing that his passion had been growing exponentially and he began to regularly contribute his poetry to well-regarded literary Urdu magazines such as *Shama*. This went down well with neither his brother nor their father; both men were puzzled and alarmed by the younger Singh's seeming insistence on self-sabotage, seeing as he was inexplicably attracted to a vocation that in their view had no future and was, therefore, a waste of time. '*Hamare ghar meerasi kahan se aa gaya?*' (How did this family produce a lowly entertainer?) Sardar Makhan Singh wondered incredulously. Regardless, Gulzar tried his best, for a time, to strike a balance between his creative calling and the demands of his family that he seek 'a stable and respectable occupation'.[5] He switched from Khalsa College to National College, where he could indulge his insatiable hunger for the treasures of Urdu and Persian literature, and he dutifully helped look after Jasmer's various business outlets. However, over time it became increasingly clear, at least to Gulzar, that this state of affairs could not continue indefinitely; his heart was not in the kind of work his brother and father deemed worthy, and they could never

---

5   Chatterjee, *Echoes & Eloquences*, p. 9.

comprehend the 'usefulness' of the work he wanted to do. Despite his best efforts, this fundamental difference in world view often resulted in showdowns at home, with Jasmer lashing out at his younger sibling in the harshest of language. Their father, too, took his older son's side, writing angry letters of admonishment to Gulzar. Matters finally came to a head when Gulzar decided to drop out of college at the end of his second year to pursue a full-time literary career. Jasmer could not abide by what he saw as not only a disastrous decision but also a personal affront. Gulzar felt he had no choice but to leave his brother's home and strike out on his own. He did so with the promise that their father would be none the wiser to this new arrangement; both brothers wanted to protect the old man from the heartache of discovering that they had fallen out so badly. Gulzar referred to this process as 'untying', as opposed to breaking away, from his family.

Finding employment and accommodation didn't take much time: he was hired as the manager of an automobile workshop and rented a room at Coover Lodge, a property owned by the famed writer Krishan Chander, who also lived there. This would prove to be a serendipitous move. After years of grappling with a familial environment dismissive of his vocational desires, Gulzar was suddenly surrounded by the crème de la crème of Bombay's literary world, ensconced in a milieu that would further inspire, instigate and nurture his talent and ambition. By his own account, it was an enriching period in his life where he had the opportunity to share ideas with many like-minded people and simply bask in the presence of so many celebrated figures. He observed Krishan Chander at work and was impressed by his tremendous sense of discipline. Sahir Ludhianvi was his neighbour at Coover Lodge – a 'friendly but moody' man[6] – and he often heard him recite at events held by the Progressive Writers' Association (PWA), an organization Gulzar had become actively involved with. The PWA also gave him the chance to meet and listen to other great writers like Majrooh Sultanpuri, Ali Sardar Jafri and Yusuf Mannan, though he confessed that, being an awestruck youth, he did not at the time have the confidence to discuss their work with them.

Gulzar's coterie of friends closer to home also helped fuel his talent. He credits Punjabi poet Sukhbir for expanding his taste to include world literature and the work of the likes of Neruda, Sartre and Auden, among others. He had known Sagar Sarhadi since their college days together and, in this new phase of life, they became each other's sounding boards, with Gulzar reciting his poetry to Sarhadi and the latter regaling him with readings of his short stories and plays. He also got on well with Balraj Sahni; their mutual love for literature and shared Punjabi background provided plenty of fodder for many sittings together. Most of Gulzar's

---

6   Gulzar and Kabir, *In the Company of a Poet*, p. 43.

friends were card-carrying communists and he found that he agreed with their ideals of equality and social justice. Though he never formally joined the Party, he has always been a proponent of the view that 'writers must be aware of what is happening in the world and have a strong sense of values. They do not have to be activists, or be actively involved in politics, but believing in some kind of ideology is essential'.[7] This humanist outlook would, of course, strongly inform his work as both a writer and a filmmaker.

It was another one of his friendships that ultimately led to Gulzar joining the Bombay film industry; something that he had not been terribly inclined towards doing and, in all likelihood, would not have done if left to his own devices. But his close friend, poet and lyricist Shailendra virtually forced him into it and he found himself unable to say no. He wrote a few film songs of little consequence under the alias of Gulzar Deenvi, but a more fruitful engagement was just around the corner. It was 1963 and Bimal Roy's latest production *Bandini* had been left without a lyricist as Shailendra had had a spat with Roy's favourite composer, S.D. Burman. Shailendra asked Debu Sen, Roy's assistant and a mutual friend of his and Gulzar's, to commission the young poet to write songs for the film. Gulzar was dismissive of the suggestion and adamant that he did not want to continue writing film songs. When Sen related this

---

7   Ibid., p. 45.

to Shailendra, the older poet admonished his young friend for his snobbish attitude. 'Do you think all film people are illiterate?' Gulzar recalled Shailendra asking him. 'People are dying to work with Bimal *da*. Go and see him!'[8]

Suitably chastised, Gulzar accompanied Debu Sen to meet the great director. When they were introduced, Bimal Roy, likely because of Gulzar's name, mistakenly thought he was Muslim and expressed concern as to how he would understand the Bengali Vaishnava poetry style that he wanted to emulate for some of the film's songs; Sen assured him that the young man was actually a fluent Bengali-speaking Punjabi Sikh. Although Gulzar ended up writing only one song for the film, Burman and Shailendra having buried the hatchet in no time, Bimal *da* had taken a liking to the poet and convinced him to give up his job at the workshop to take up a position as his assistant instead, even suggesting at this early juncture that he could eventually turn director himself. Gulzar accepted and the song he had written for *Bandini*, the enchanting '*Mora gora ang lai le*' (at whose recording he also met Lata Mangeshkar for the first time), became tremendously popular. His film journey in Bombay had begun in earnest.

His relationship with Bimal Roy was not only professionally fortuitous but also one of mutual respect and admiration that belonged to a bygone era, as Gulzar himself

8   Ibid., p. 50.

describes it. Sadly, it was to last only a few precious years as Bimal *da* grew progressively sick with cancer, eventually dying in January 1965. It was a devastating loss for his protégé, who felt 'as though I had lost my father all over again'.[9] At this difficult time, singer-composer Hemant Kumar made sure that the members of the late director's unit did not lose their professional footing in the industry in the wake of their mentor's demise. As it happened, he was composing the music for Asit Sen's Waheeda Rehman-Rajesh Khanna starrer *Khamoshi* (1970) and he managed to persuade the director to hire Gulzar to write not only the songs but also the screenplay. Around the same time, he introduced the poet to Hrishikesh Mukherjee, who had turned director some years earlier after a rewarding stint as Bimal *da*'s editor and assistant. The two hit it off immediately and Hrishi *da* asked Gulzar to come on board as the screenwriter and lyricist for his latest production, *Aashirwad*. Two years later, they again worked together on *Anand* and *Guddi* (1971). The producer of *Anand* was a gentleman by the name of N.C. Sippy who, in the same year, gave Gulzar his break as a director.

Gulzar had been keen on making a film himself since his days with Bimal *da* and he had learnt a great deal about the art of filmmaking from the late auteur. So, when filmmaker Tapan Sinha abandoned the idea of directing

---

9   Ibid., p. 64.

the Hindi version of his Bengali film *Apanjan* (1968) for N.C. Sippy, Gulzar dropped his name into the hat for potential directors. 'Once you understand how to make an omelette you have to break the eggs, don't you?' he reasoned.[10] It was his script, after all, so he felt confident that he could pull it off as well as anyone else. Sippy was intrigued by the idea but did not acquiesce immediately, instead telling Gulzar to come for a meeting to his home at four in the morning, the unearthly hour at which the producer always started his day. Though an early riser himself, the aspiring director still found it daunting to make it to his potential benefactor's place on time. But make it he did, thereby convincing Sippy that he was serious about his endeavours and, therefore, the right choice for the job. He did warn Gulzar, though, that Hrishikesh Mukherjee, Sippy's business partner and usually his default choice as director on any of their projects, would have to give his approval. Needless to say, that approval was granted without hesitation and Gulzar took his position in the director's chair for the first time. The film was *Mere Apne* (1971).

The cinematic journey that began on this sweet note would hit few, if any, sour notes in the years and decades to come. From the beginning, Gulzar's was a singular voice, developing a brand of cinema that was all his own: a happy

---

10 Ibid., p. 84.

marriage between elements of neorealism and traditional commercial storytelling. Like other filmmakers of the auteurist bent, Gulzar, too, organically came to inhabit all the major roles responsible for designing and controlling the making of a film, a fact he readily acknowledges: 'In my films I try to do everything I can – writing the script, the lyrics, the dialogue and directing. For those things I cannot do, I turn to others but I tell the cinematographer exactly what I want to see ... the angle of a shot, the light. In this way, I indulge in every part of the production. For example, I control the actor. I tell him or her that I want a tear to form in the eye but not to let it fall. Hold that tear. Keep holding it there on the rim of your eye. Only when I say, should you let it run down your cheek'.[11]

It was in his seventeenth year as a director, with a critically and commercially acclaimed body of work already behind him, that Gulzar came to make *Ijaazat*.

---

11 Stephen Alter, *Fantasies of a Bollywood Love Thief: Inside the World of Indian Moviemaking*, New Delhi: HarperCollins Publishers, 2007, p. 81.

chapter two

Chhoti Si Kahani Se

The Story

☙

A train comes to a halt at a dimly lit, non-descript railway station in the middle of a stormy night. Mahendra (Naseeruddin Shah) alights and makes his way to the musty waiting room to await the morning train. Another passenger in the room – a woman – is startled to see him and hides behind a magazine. But the subterfuge cannot last for long and, soon enough, the two come face to face. The woman is Sudha (Rekha). As the night progresses and they tentatively delve into conversation, the story of their shared past unfolds through haunting vignettes.

Years ago, Mahendra had been promised in marriage to Sudha, a teacher at a local school in Panchgani and the daughter of his grandfather, Dadu's (Shammi Kapoor) ward Parvati (Sulabha Deshpande). But in the intervening years, living and working as a photographer in the city, faraway from the rural milieu of his family, Mahendra had secretly made a life with the free-spirited poet Maya (Anuradha Patel), with the two sharing a house out of wedlock. Things come to a head when Dadu presses Mahendra to set a date for the wedding. In desperation, Mahendra confesses all to Sudha, who tells him to come clean and take Maya to meet his grandfather; to do what is truthful and right. But Maya, unpredictable and impulsive, has pulled one of her regular disappearing acts and is nowhere to be found. Feeling cornered, and lacking the courage to tell Dadu the truth, Mahendra marries Sudha.

The two attempt to make a life together; Mahendra making an earnest effort to put his past, and his thoughts of Maya, behind him and Sudha asking for little more than the small joys of traditional marriage. But traces of Maya keep clouding their life together: her photograph in Mahendra's wallet, her belongings in a suitcase left behind and, overwhelmed by loneliness, her occasional phone calls to Mahendra. Sudha, her protestations notwithstanding, feels sympathy for the younger woman's heartbreak and obvious need for emotional stability. When Mahendra returns Maya's belongings upon Sudha's urging, she sends a poem back to him in response, asking him to also send the things he forgot: the intangible *objets de mémoire* (objects of memory) that embody their time together, which can only be felt and remembered. For how does one return memories? '*Mera kuch saaman tumhare paas pada hai ...*' (Some of my belongings are still with you ...). Sudha is racked with guilt.

For her part, Maya, too, expresses no anger or resentment towards Sudha – only awe and respect. She does not want to break up their home, but to have some small, undefined part in it. However, despite the soft corner she has for her, Sudha's pride will not allow her to give up that space. While she and Mahendra are away on their honeymoon, Maya attempts suicide and ends up in hospital. Mahendra does not tell Sudha about this but, unable to help himself, starts meeting Maya again in secret, knowing that she needs him in her fragile state. Torn between the two women, he finds himself in an impossible situation from which there appears to be no escape. It's plain to Sudha that he is preoccupied and that a chasm is growing between them. When she confronts him about his rekindled relationship, he proposes that he bring Maya to the house and they try to find a solution together. Sudha bristles at the suggestion, insisting that she doesn't want to meet Maya, but Mahendra calls Maya on the phone anyway and makes it seem as if Sudha has put forth the invitation. Maya's joy at the request is short-lived when she hears Sudha in the background, angrily reproaching Mahendra for lying.

With Mahendra gone to pacify Maya, Sudha quietly abandons both the house and the relationship, leaving only a brief note behind. She returns to Panchgani and confides in her old principal, Mrs. Khariwala (Dina Pathak), that she intends to file for a divorce and take up a teaching position at a school faraway, having lost hope for a reconciliation since Mahendra made no attempt to contact her. Unbeknownst to her, Mahendra has suffered a heart attack upon reading her farewell note. Maya nurses him back to health and the two appear to return to their old life. Then, one day, a letter arrives from Sudha, stating that she is granting Mahendra a divorce.

Back in the waiting room, five years after her departure from their home, Sudha asks after Maya. Mahendra tells her all he had kept hidden before – Maya's attempted suicide, his meeting her to make her feel secure, his own heart attack – and the final devastating revelation: Maya is long dead, having been killed in an accident. Seeing Mahendra's shattered reaction on receiving Sudha's letter, she had, impulsively and clumsily, attempted to instigate a reconciliation between them. Mahendra aggressively told her off and Maya, unable to stomach the fight and the toxicity of the situation, rode off on her motorbike in the middle of the night. Before Mahendra could catch up with her, her long scarf got entangled in the wheels of the bike, breaking her neck and killing her instantly. Sudha is overcome with shock and grief.

Many moments pass wordlessly as dawn breaks. Mahendra notes that Sudha hasn't said anything about her life of the last five years. She states simply that there isn't anything much to tell but does mention that her mother has passed away. With a note of hope in his voice and on his visage, Mahendra asks whether that means she is alone. Before she can reply, a man (Shashi Kapoor) bursts through the door and addresses Sudha with great familiarity. As he chatters on animatedly, it slowly dawns on Mahendra that the man is her husband; Sudha has remarried.

Left alone in the waiting room for a moment, Mahendra and Sudha face each other in silence. She expresses her regret at having left him without asking the last time and tearfully asks him to grant her permission to leave this time ('*Pichhli baar bina poochhe chali gayi thi. Iss baar ijaazat de do*'). He gives her his blessings and asks for her forgiveness. Sudha's husband reappears in the doorway just as she bends down to touch Mahendra's feet. He is puzzled but realizes quickly who the man is and gives a gentle, understanding smile in response.

Mahendra, left alone on the platform, watches them walk away.

chapter three

Mera Kuch Saaman

The Making, the Memories

ℭℛ

'I read the story by Subodh Ghosh, whom I call the Maupassant of Bengali literature.'

It is intriguing that Gulzar would make that connection between the twentieth-century Bengali writer behind the narrative of *Ijaazat* (based on his short story *Jatugriha*) and the nineteenth-century French author known for his gripping, laconic prose. Over a period of barely ten years, Guy de Maupassant had produced 300 short stories, 200 articles, six novels, two plays and three travel books. In his own words, he saw life as 'brutal, incoherent, disjointed, full of inexplicable, illogical and contradictory disasters'.[12] He had

---

12 Chris Power, 'A brief survey of the short story part 49: Guy de Maupassant', *The Guardian*, 2013, https://www.theguardian.com/

an affinity for seamy details that were at once grotesque and fascinating, once describing the scene of a Parisian park as a Fellini-esque nightmare:

> Busty women with peroxided hair and nipped-in waists could be seen, made up to the nines with blood red lips and black-kohled eyes. Tightly laced into their garish dresses they trailed in all their vulgar glory over the fresh green grass. They were accompanied by men whose fashion-plate accessories, light gloves, patent-leather boots, canes as slender as threads and absurd monocles made them look like complete idiots. (*Femme Fatale* 1881)

Although the quality of his body of work is often uneven, there can be no doubt as to the enormous influence Maupassant had on the countless writers who have followed in his steps, most significantly in the realm of short story writing. From Hemingway to Raymond Carver, Isaac Babel to Henry James, all of them owe at least some degree of debt to the Frenchman. James said of his harsh naturalism, 'He fixes a hard eye on some spot of human life,

---

books/booksblog/2013/may/24/survey-short-story-guy-de-maupassant, accessed on 29 November 2018.

usually some dreary, ugly, shabby, sordid one, takes up the particle, and squeezes it either till it grimaces or bleeds.'[13]

Like Maupassant, Subodh Ghosh is renowned for his prolific output in Bengali short story writing, in addition to his humanist outlook and vast knowledge of tribal cultures of India. Although his most popular literary work is probably *Bharat Premkatha*, a retelling of the romantic tales from the *Mahabharata*, his oeuvre traverses a vast and varied range of subjects and emotional planes. He stated that he drew upon his experiences as 'a circus-performer, bus conductor, hotel-manager, mica-mining prospector, confectioner, butter merchant, sadhu, political worker, district-board health inspector, poultry farmer, and union volunteer' for his stories.[14] But whatever the topic, Ghosh remains squarely focussed on one overarching concern: the fragile complexity of human relationships, not only between two people but between their surroundings and themselves. Perhaps that is one of the reasons why he has proven to be a popular choice for filmmakers, many of whom have adapted his works to the screen. It was his

---

13 In Power, 'A brief survey of the short story part 49: Guy de Maupassant'.

14 Anirban, 'Of failed marriages, waiting rooms, and cups of tea', *Milkmiracle*, 3 July 2013, https://milkmiracle.net/2013/07/03/of-failed-marriages-waiting-rooms-and-cups-of-tea/, accessed on 29 November 2018.

stories that formed the basis for Bimal Roy's *Anjangarh* (1948) and *Sujata* (1960), the latter of which won Ghosh a Filmfare Award for Best Story, as well as Ritwik Ghatak's critically acclaimed masterpiece *Ajantrik* (1958). Mrinal Sen's 1972 film *Ek Adhuri Kahani* was based on *Gotrantar*, while Basu Chatterjee's popular hit *Chitchor* (1976) was an adaptation of *Chittachakor*. Even *Jatugriha* had been filmed by Tapan Sinha under the same title in 1964.

As for Gulzar's encounter with the story: 'I came upon the book at [actor] Abhi Bhattacharya's house. I was working for Bimal *da* at the time and had learned to read Bengali recently. I was startled when I read it; I thought it was a beautiful story. I mentioned it to Abhi *da* and he told me he was in college when the story was first published. Now that was a time when writing romantic fiction was *de rigueur*. So, when this story came out, as Abhi *da* put it, "*Meri* centre wicket *ud gayi!*" (I was bowled over). I read other stories from the same book as well, like *Olik Babu*. Later on, I acquired the rights for both *Olik Babu* and *Jatugriha* from Subodh *da*.'

Of course, this was not the first time that Gulzar had turned to a literary source for cinematic inspiration. From the beginning of his directorial career, he had gravitated towards novels and short stories for mining narrative material and his own background often helped in persuading the authors in question to grant permission for their works to be adapted. That was certainly the case when he requested

K.A. Abbas's approval for adapting his Urdu short story *Dil Hi To Hai* to the big screen, ultimately released under the title *Achanak* in 1973. Among others, *Khushboo* was based on the classic Bengali novel *Panditmashai* by Sarat Chandra Chattopadhyay (filmed in the original language in 1951 by Naresh Mitra), while both *Kitaab* (1977) and *Namkeen* (1982) were adapted from stories by Bengali author Samaresh Basu. At the time that Gulzar first toyed with the idea of adapting *Jatugriha*, the world of Hindi films had evolved into one where such stories were warily viewed as unsellable. The director recalls: 'This was the time in Hindi cinema when you'd have a hero and a heroine who would bump into each other on bicycles and he'd help her pick up her fallen books and both would then proceed to fall in love. That was the idea of romance! One didn't see mature characters or love stories. This was frustrating because working with Bimal Roy, one had seen films being made that were based on literature and each character was so detailed, like fine threads woven into a tapestry. For example, on *Bandini*, I remember there was a great debate about how Kalyani could not go out of the house at night; she was a village girl, so she couldn't go out and start singing '*Mora gora ang lai le*'. But Sachin Dev Burman was adamant; he said the music he had composed for the song had to be picturized outdoors against the night sky or its effect would be dampened. Bimal *da* was equally insistent that the girl could not go and sing outside at night.

Suddenly, Paul Mahendra, one of our senior writing assistants, spoke up and said, "*Dada*, would a young girl sing Vaishnava *kavita* inside the house where her father is sleeping nearby? Wouldn't she feel awkward?" And Burman *da's* reaction was priceless – "*Ayi leyo*! Will she or won't she go outside to sing now?" Imagine, two senior artists spending so much time arguing over one situation! So, the school of thought I had worked with and learned from paid great attention to the intricacies of character.'

The title of the story – *Jatugriha* – translates to '*Lac ka Ghar*' or 'The Lac House' and is a reference to the pivotal *Lakshagraha* chapter from the *Mahabharata*. In this episode, the dastardly Kauravas trick their cousins, the righteous Pandavas, into staying in a house made out of highly flammable lac in the forest of Varnavrat, the aim being to set the house alight and have the Pandavas burn to death. But, thanks to their uncle Vidura, the Pandavas are warned well in time and escape the burning building through an underground escape route. In Subodh Ghosh's story, the lac house became the railway station waiting room where the once-married couple, Satadal and Madhuri, meet by chance and are forced to face each other, the failure of their marriage and their failings as individuals. 'What was most compelling for me,' remembers Gulzar, 'was the scenario where two strangers meet at a railway platform. But, of course, they're not strangers at all, as we learn, but were once husband and wife and are now meeting again years later.'

From the pioneering film by the Lumière Brothers (*Arrival of a Train*, 1895) and the romantic classic by David Lean (*Brief Encounter*, 1945), to the grit and glamour of Bollywood epics (*Sholay* and *Dilwale Dulhaniya Le Jayenge*, 1995); from the doomed romanticism of Tolstoy's *Anna Karenina* to the psychological violence of Émile Zola's *La Bête Humaine*, trains and train stations have always held a certain fascination for filmmakers and writers alike and have featured significantly as locations across every era. In *Jatugriha*, Subodh Ghosh sets the stage as thus:

> *This was the Rajpur Railway Station, not a court. Here there were no judges, no lawyers, no witnesses, no lines formed by unblinking, judgemental eyes. There were no devious lines of inquiry by an appointed third party simply because there were no secrets to be unearthed. Still, the secluded familiarity of being together in the same waiting room was suffocating. It would have been nice to have escaped: it would have been proper to have escaped.*[15]

The original story differed in many significant ways from what eventually made its way to the screen. 'It was of a bygone world and values, of course,' explains Gulzar. 'In it, the character of the "other woman" was a sewing teacher. The man who falls in love with her [Satadal] is already

---

15 Anirban, 'Of failed marriages, waiting rooms, and cups of tea'.

married and one of the problems in the marriage is that the couple are unable to have a child. One of the modern aspects of the story was that the wife refuses to accept that the lack of a child is her "fault" and she challenges the husband to get himself tested since it could just as easily be some issue with him. Then they part, he marries the sewing teacher, etc.'

Part of the reason why the story went through significant changes was the amount of time that lapsed between when Gulzar first bought the rights from the author and when he was able to find financial backing for it. The director recalls: 'I bought the story from Subodh *da*, who was quite elderly by the time I got to know him, and started working on it. The working title was "Departure". But nobody wanted to make a film in which the heroine was a married woman! Mr. Sippy told me that a heroine getting married at the end of a film was fine, but who'd watch a film in which she was already "taken" when the story starts? So the project got stalled, though I continued to tinker with it and update it as time went on and our values evolved.'

One of the major changes was in the development of the character of the 'other woman', who was a minor character mentioned only in passing as Satadal's current wife in the original story. Gulzar wanted more contemporary elements in the story to authentically reflect the times and Maya was created, fashioned as a free-spirited '80s flower child who becomes the sticking point in Mahendra and Sudha's marriage. The issue of infertility was omitted altogether. Significantly, another addition to the screen version was the matter-of-fact suggestion of Maya and Mahendra living together without being married to each other. Gulzar wanted to include this because 'I found the concept of a live-in relationship – something new at that time – very pleasant and refreshing. One saw it at the Poona Institute, because boys and girls who studied there lived together like friends and colleagues in the same hostels; there was no separation of the sexes. They were working people, equals. So I also added an angle to Maya's character that she ran away from home to become an actress at FTII, met this man, fell in love and moved in with him.'

The filmmaker knew that he was getting further and further away from Ghosh's plot and characters, but he didn't give it much thought over the years because the eventuality of actually finding funding for the film seemed remote. It was a treasured project but, at the back of his mind, he had reconciled himself to the possibility that it might never see the light of day and would just sit gathering dust in the back of a cupboard for posterity. And then, out of the blue, 'Many years later, I found someone who was willing to produce it. I went to Subodh *da* to get his blessing, and I was nervous because by this time the story had changed a great deal.' Gulzar was especially anxious because he was aware that the writer's reaction to the earlier Bengali adaptation of the story had not been a particularly positive one. Even though Tapan Sinha himself was under the impression that Ghosh had liked his screen retelling of *Jatugriha* – 'He was very pleased,' the filmmaker stated in an interview in 1991 – the author had expressed his disappointment to Gulzar: 'He had told me once before that he was unhappy with Tapan Sinha's version of *Jatugriha*, that Tapan didn't understand the story.' Knowing this, Gulzar felt himself to be in a fairly tenuous position. 'Because of this and other similar experiences, Subodh *da* didn't have much confidence in filmmakers,' he remembers. 'He felt they took material from literature but changed it liberally to suit their own requirements. And here I was, having changed the characters and everything else other than the basic premise of the chance meeting at the railway station!'

So it was, understandably, with considerable trepidation that Gulzar approached Subodh Ghosh to apprise him of the shape that his story had taken. He started by stating that he had made 'a few changes'. At this, the older man displayed no emotion and simply asked for a narration. 'So, I started narrating it,' says Gulzar. 'I could tell from his expressions that he knew his story was gone. But he listened in silence. I think nothing surprises a veteran writer; they have too much life experience to be taken aback by anything. I finished my narration and waited pensively for his reaction. After a pause, he said, "It's not that story [that I wrote], but it sounds good." As soon as he said that I was immensely relieved and asked him if he would agree to be credited as the author of the story. If he hadn't I couldn't have made the film, but luckily, he did. "After all," he said, "you've paid me for it." Then I took over the film as totally my own rendering; I made the characters my own.'

It is the richness of his characters that has always made Gulzar's films so distinctive. As it happened, *Ijaazat* still took time getting off the ground (Subodh Ghosh passed away in the intervening years), and the filmmaker took this time to hone the script and refine the characters further. 'The smallest details are there in the script,' he asserts. 'From the way a character might hold a cup of tea to the way he heaves a sigh. I include even the smallest actions in the script – "he leaned on the sofa and looked up as she walked in" – that sort of thing. So, the whole film, with all its intricacies of characters, is there on the page.'

This detailing of character is something that is explored and expressed with great delicacy by Gulzar as the writer, with many instances where the poeticism of the dialogue emerges from a combination of how turns of phrase are fashioned and how they are employed in the narrative context. When Sudha and Mahendra finally start talking in the waiting room after the initial awkwardness, she asks him if he still lives in the same place they once shared – '*Wahin rehte hain aap?*' (Do you still live there?). He replies in the affirmative, going on to say: '*Wohi sheher hai, wohi gali, wohi ghar. Sab kuch … wohi to nahin hai, lekin hai wahin.*' (The same town, the same lane, the same house. Everything ... isn't the same, but it's still there). This lyrical idea of places and time held frozen in a haze of memories is reminiscent of the same expressed by Pablo Neruda in his celebrated Love Sonnet IV:

> *That time was like never*
> *and like always*
> *So we go there*
> *where nothing is waiting*
> *We find everything*
> *waiting there.*

In another exchange between them, Mahendra notes that Sudha now wears spectacles:

M: *'Acha lagta hai. Samajhdar lagti ho.'*
(It looks nice. You look wise.)

S: *'Paanch saal pehle samajhdar nahin lagti thi?'*
(I didn't look wise five years ago?)

M: *'Nahin, lagti thi. Ab zyada lagti ho.'*
(No, you did. Now you look wiser.)

S: *'Aapne daadhi kab se badha li?'*
(How long have you had the beard?)

M: *'Kuch dinon se. Kyun, samajhdar nahin lagta?'*
(A few days. Why? Don't I look wise?)

'They are sharing the missing years,' Gulzar elaborates, 'and they are weighing the changes. But after everything is said and done, we have to wonder: have they really changed? Have they really "grown up"? Maybe those physical changes are the only changes that have taken place because the relationship is still very much there.' Certainly, the seemingly innocuous and casual nature of the conversation barely conceals the familiarity that the two are tentatively finding their way towards. At the same time, it serves as a reminder that this familiarity comes from underlying emotional wounds that these cosmetic changes and accoutrements of wisdom cannot mask. But even in the act of rediscovering the hurt, there are hints of the undeniable power their relationship has over them. Mahendra is contrite after yelling at Sudha when she trips and hurts her leg when the lights go out in the waiting room. He explains his outburst as a force of habit that the years of separation cannot eradicate – *'aadat nahin jaati'* (some habits don't go away). Sudha has a deeper reading of the emotions at play: *'Aadat bhi chali jaati hai, adhikar nahin jaate'* (habits go away, entitlement doesn't). Gulzar agrees that this exchange denotes the idea that the past is always alive in the present. 'The very fact that they can argue like that leads organically to the dialogue about habits,' he states.

'The argument is symbolic of their bond which is emerging again. Where disputes once drove them apart, now they're bringing them close. Even shouting freely at each other is a sign of love between two people, because there is no need for pretence or false politeness.'

The subtext of the dynamics in the waiting room are summed up by Gulzar in one beautifully perceptive line of dialogue. When Mahendra observes that the rain is coming down harder outside and wonders when it will stop, Sudha says simply, '*Jab baras jayegi to aap hi tham jayegi*' ('It'll stop when it has poured enough'). Gulzar concurs that 'this is a very meaningful line, not a throwaway. It's not about the rain at all; it's about the two of them.' The notion that all that has been unsaid, all the pain and regret that has not been articulated, cannot remain so if there is to be healing and forgiveness is one that is central to the theme of the film.

CR

The production of *Ijaazat* was a long and often arduous one, and so the memories associated with it run the gamut from pleasant and inspiring to tedious and infuriating but Gulzar prefers not to dwell on the latter. Instead, he remembers the highlights with affection and the nadirs with humour, keeping the perspective that it is ultimately all a learning experience. He is particularly nostalgic about the one major outdoor spell that was undertaken for the film: 'Part of the song "*Katra katra*" was to be picturized at the lake at Kudremukh. In the lake, you have these trees which rot and die because of the ore in the soil and, when that happens, their tops are chopped off by the area authorities and all you see are leafless trees with darkened trunks and ragged branches. They look more like sculptures than trees. I even wrote a poem about the sight of those trees later ...

> *Kudremukh ki jheel mein*
> *Paerr nangay budh bhakshu-on ke jaise sar munday*
> *Ghutno ghutno paani mein kharray huay*
> *Haath uttha ke be-swaad aasman ki taraf*
> *Pukartay hain usko jiska, ghar wahan kahin nahin!*

(Trees stand sedate,
Serene as Buddhist monks in prayer
Knee deep in water, arms raised
To a sky too clear
Calling out for one who does not reside there.)

– Pluto, 47

The Kudremukh (Horse-Face) National Park, as it was designated in 1987, is a UNESCO heritage sight in the Chikmagalur district in Karnataka. While today it consists of rolling green hills and lush fertile forests full of diverse flora and fauna, three decades ago the landscape bore the adverse effects of a large strip mining operation by the Kudremukh

Iron Ore Company Limited. The activities of the company had led to vast deforestation, destruction of wildlife and unfettered siltation of the rivers and reservoirs. Despite these environmental ravages, Gulzar saw a haunting beauty in the starkness of the scenery that would be reflective of his characters' internal landscapes. This penchant for using locations as visual representatives of emotional terrains had found voice earlier, too, of course; perhaps most notably in *Kinara*. In the 1977 film, the melancholic longing of the song '*Naam gum jayega*' was rendered even more evocative by the location Gulzar chose for its picturization: the stunning ruins of Mandu in Madhya Pradesh. '[Here] the walls of bricks and bodies have fallen,' he muses, 'but the love of Baz Bahadur and Roopmati has survived ... When I was writing this song, the location was very much alive in my mind.'[16]

Although the sequence at Kudremukh did not require extensive shooting, the shots themselves were complicated to capture for a number reasons. Gulzar explains: 'In the early hours of the morning, there's a heavy mist in the area and on the surface of the lake, which disperses once the sun emerges fully. The only way to capture the beauty of that mist, and how it slowly starts to move and lift as the first rays of the sun hit the water, was to shoot there at four or five in the morning. So, I told Naseer and Rekha that we

---

16 Gulzar, *100 Lyrics*, New Delhi: Penguin Viking, 2009, p. 153.

were to shoot there before dawn and that I'd be there with our cameraman, Ashok Mehta, with everything set up and ready to go.

'Now, Rekha has the habits of a pandit (priest); she's the kind of person who wakes up at four in the morning and does yoga. Naseer, on the other hand, is hardly an early riser. "Bhai, that'll be very difficult," he grumbled. "You're asking a lot. I want the rest of the day off to sleep then." I agreed and said that after we had the shots, I'd give the rest of the day off to the whole unit, whether they wanted to sleep, shop, sightsee, or whatever.

'So, they both arrived at four, Rekha having made sure Naseer woke up and got ready on time, a task that I had entrusted her with. We also had a few police constables around for security purposes, which was usual on location shoots. We set up one of the shots, with both of them ready on their marks, and were waiting for the first rays of the sun. Just when we were about to roll, some man came running up into the frame to demand Naseer and Rekha's autographs! There was a mad dash as everybody went to pick him up and physically remove him – "Where has this idiot come from?!" It was just a moment of inconvenience, of course, but at the time it was a moment of absolute crisis, though not completely unexpected because people see film equipment being carried somewhere and they're bound to follow the trail. But thank God, we did finally manage to get the shot, as well as a few others. And in the end, it was worth it because the scene looked like an abstract painting.'

Other issues that cropped up were more banal but no less exasperating for Gulzar's creative spirit: 'At one point, while we were still at Kudremukh, a rift developed between the producer [R.K. Gupta] and his partner. Shooting came to a halt. Shammi Kapoorji came to try to sort the matter out but they wouldn't listen. So, I said to them, "If you feel you can't part with your money for the production, please stay in your hotel rooms; I'll find the money myself and finish the shoot." Finally, they realized that it wasn't right to stall the whole film because of their differences and told me to go ahead, there wouldn't be any problems on set. That was such a mundane moment; every shoot has its share of those.'

Then there were the happier moments and these are memories that the filmmaker recalls with fondness: 'There is a little *shararat* that I added to the opening titles. If you watch the film, you'll note that when the song '*Chhoti si kahani se*' finishes, all the titles have come and gone except for my director's credit. During a trial show, my editor thought I'd forgotten to put my own credit! The opening scene starts, Mahendra is about to get off the train and he shouts, "Coolie!" And that's when my name finally appears on the screen, in response to "coolie". So sometimes you have these moments of mischief also. Another little anecdote to do with the titles: Ram Mohan, who played the station master, came to me after the trial show and said, "I think there's a mistake in my credit, it says Ram Mohanji." I told him that I knew; I thought I'd list him onscreen by what we called him offscreen! It's all in fun. When you work so closely as a team, you can do things like this. It warms the heart to remember them.'

Crucial to the overall experience of a film, for both the filmmaker and the audience, is, of course, the cast of actors assembled to tell the story. As a director, Gulzar describes this process of selecting his performers as something that happens quite organically: 'Once the script is written and you read it back a few times, it's first the body language of the characters that starts to form in your mind, much more than their faces. You see these gestures, how a character sits, uses his hands, etc. Once that takes concrete form, the faces start falling into place as well. So, in fact, one casts actors according to body language and not so much the face.'

It is worthwhile to take a look at the astuteness with which Gulzar cast some of the minor but important roles in *Ijaazat*. Rita Rani Kaul, already familiar to audiences for playing Ramdei in Muzaffar Ali's production of *Umrao Jaan* (1981), played Maya's friend Mona, bringing an urbane sophistication to the small part with her somewhat anglicized looks and enunciation. As noted earlier, senior character actor Ram Mohan was cast as the kindly station master. His comforting, old-world presence had been utilized by Gulzar earlier in *Kitaab*, *Namkeen* and *Angoor*.

Sudha's old school principal was played by another familiar and popular face: Dina Pathak, who, by that time, was also Naseeruddin Shah's mother-in-law as the actor had married her daughter Ratna in the early 1980s. Gulzar named the character Mrs Khariwala 'after the headmistress of Bosky's school! She was a great headmistress.'

For the role of Sudha's mother, Parvati, Gulzar called upon the late Sulabha Deshpande, doyenne of Marathi and Hindi theatre and respected character actor of many acclaimed films, including Shyam Benegal's *Bhumika* (1977), Saeed Mirza's *Albert Pinto Ko Ghussa Kyun Aata Hai* (1980) and Sagar Sarhadi's *Bazaar* (1982). Although the part is small, the actor makes it memorable by playing it with her trademark nervy quality. Gulzar is especially fond of how she made the character vaguely neurotic: 'She keeps crying at the drop of a hat!' In one scene, when Dadu suggests that she ask Sudha whether she wants to marry Mahendra or not, Parvati replies, '*Uss se kya poochna, aap ki charan dhuli to woh aankhon se lagaati hai*' (There's no need to ask her when she worships the ground you walk on). It is to the actor's credit that the deference in the line comes across as sympathetic and heavy with pathos, rather than merely obsequious.

For the part of Sudha's second husband, who only appears in the film's final scene, Gulzar knew he needed a star; a random actor would not do. 'I wanted to justify Rekha's going away with him,' he states. 'An unknown person wouldn't have balanced the presence of Rekha and Naseer.'[17] Although Shashi Kapoor's career as a leading man was winding down by the time *Ijaazat* came to be made, his was still a formidable name in the film world, especially as India's first true-blue crossover star who had worked extensively in many western films. He was also a greatly respected producer of independent films. 'I narrated the story to [him],' Gulzar remembers. 'As I narrated, he kept asking me, "What am I doing in this film?" I could see from his expression that he wouldn't do it. But the moment I narrated the scene where he opens the door and enters the waiting room, like a loving husband, I could see his facial expression change. And he promptly said, "I'll do it." His presence helped the scene so much.'[18] Certainly, the actor's familiar effervescence and breezy charm fits the role and its requirements like a glove. He made it utterly believable that a husband, confronted with his wife's past, is mature and secure enough in himself to take it in his stride instead of turning it into a moment of crisis. It is, in fact, a part that is reminiscent of the one he played in Yash Chopra's *Kabhi Kabhie* (1976) and he performed both with aplomb. But he wasn't the only Kapoor cast in the film.

The tallest of the Kapoor elders, at over six feet, who as a young boy had a fascination for Errol Flynn movies

17 Shalini Razdan, 'Gulzar on Ijaazat?', newsgroups.derkeiler, 19 June 2006.

18 Ibid.

and who had started smoking in his teens to gruff up his thin voice, Shamsher Raj had become Hindi cinema's dancing superstar in the 1960s under his family pet name of Shammi. In his private life, he was a voracious reader and lived life to the fullest, enjoying good food, copious amounts of drinks and the company of women. He was known and loved for his joie de vivre and generosity of spirit. Widowed at a young age after the death of his wife Geeta Bali in 1965, Shammi Kapoor slowly lost interest in playing the romantic and let himself go, piling on weight and eventually growing out his hair and beard. In this new avatar, he began an entirely new chapter in his acting career – that of a beloved character actor. Gulzar knew Shammi Kapoor was the ideal choice for the role of Dadu.

'Dadu's character is there to remind the audience that we are still bound by certain traditions and there's no escaping them,' Gulzar posits, 'which is why Mahendra is unable to speak up about Maya in front of him. He makes excuses about the date of the wedding but Dadu simply says, "You come when you can and I'll perform the ceremony myself." That last point also resonated with people, I believe; the fact that Dadu doesn't believe in pandits and priests and all that. So he may be traditional but he's also progressive.' And Shammi Kapoor inhabited the role completely. Gulzar recalls: 'Once we had discussed the script and his part, I didn't have to tell him anything again; when he was in front of the camera, he was Dadu, from how he spoke to the way he walked or wore the *gamcha* (cotton towel) on his head. It looked effortless. I don't know how he did it, but he just landed so smoothly into the part. Look at the part where he takes Naseer by the neck; only a Dadu can do that!'

In fact, theirs had been a long and loving friendship, one that Gulzar talks about with great affection: 'I was Shammi Kapoorji's pet! He's the one who taught me how to drink, during the making of *Andaz* (1971). I was the writer of the film and we were on location in Manali. Now Shammiji was a complete *saeen* (dervish) kind of person. He would sit outside by the fire, waiting for his shot, where he would have his make-up done and everything. I arrived one morning to see him sitting and having his usual beer. I said to him, "Shammiji, just looking at you with that cold beer in your hand in this cold weather, I start freezing!" And he said to me, in Punjabi, "*Kaka*ji, come here, sit with me and have a swig." Now it's not as though I hadn't tried it before; I'd even had *tharra* (moonshine)! But I wasn't a drinker, at most I'd have a polite sip or two in drinking company. I said to him, "Shammiji, I feel cold just looking at you drink, how can I drink it myself?" "Oh *putta*rji," he reiterated, "you have to chase *this* with the beer." And saying that, he brought out a bottle of cognac that I hadn't spotted before. Then he explained that I had to take a sip of the cognac from the bottle-cap without swallowing, chase that with a swig of beer and swallow both together! So I did and it worked! Then he'd call me over in the evening and teach me how to drink whiskey. "Forget this soda nonsense," he'd say. "You can't even taste the whiskey. And if it's the soda you want to taste, just drink that; don't waste the whiskey!" *Mast aadmi tha* (he was a unique man). He lived every moment to the fullest. I have been close to all the Kapoors and to me he was the tallest of them all, in every way. I already told you he was a *saeen* and, when he retired, he famously started wearing a mala (prayer beads) too. "I've closed up shop," he told me. "*Ho gayi* acting" (I'm done with acting). That was Shammiji.'

But, more than anything else, the success of the narrative depends on the three main characters who form the triangle at the heart of the story and the actors who play them.

chapter four

Aarzu Mein Behne Do

Maya

❧

In October 2005, director Cameron Crowe's new film *Elizabethtown* opened to tepid reviews and negligible box-office. Two years later, popular entertainment website The A.V. Club's resident critic Nathan Rabin wrote about the film's failure in his column 'My Year of Flops' and coined the term 'Manic Pixie Dream Girl' to describe the character played by Kirsten Dunst, a lovably kooky fantasy figure 'who exists solely in the fevered imaginations of sensitive writer-directors to teach broodingly soulful young men to embrace life and its infinite mysteries and adventures'.[19]

---

19 Stephanie Zacharek, 'Nonfiction: My Year of Flops: The A.V. Club Presents One Man's Journey Deep into the Heart of Cinematic Failure. By Nathan Rabin', *The New York Times Book Review*, 13, 2010.

The term, which seemed to adequately capture both the impossibly whimsical and inherently sexist nature of the popular archetype, has since become a familiar one with many film commentators employing it to criticize film tropes involving adorable, flighty, apparently emancipated women who nonetheless seem 'less like autonomous, independent entities than appealing props to help mopey, sad men self-actualize'.[20] Rabin, and others, further identified the MPDG as a very particular male fantasy: a woman with no needs, desires or complications of her own, therefore ready, willing and able to act simply as a breezy cipher for the man's escape from ennui and his own ordinariness.

Cinema has, of course, had an enduring love affair with the MPDG. Long before Rabin came up with the term, we had Katharine Hepburn as daffy heiress Susan Vance who created havoc for Cary Grant's stuffy palaeontologist in *Bringing Up Baby* (1938) and taught him to live and love in the process. Later, Audrey Hepburn in *Breakfast at Tiffany's* (1961), Ali McGraw in *Love Story* (1970), Diane Keaton in *Annie Hall* (1977) and even septuagenarian Ruth Gordon in *Harold and Maude* (1971) seemed to be essaying versions of the same idealized life-lover bringing notions of untethered freedom and joy into the lives of their hitherto deflated men. In Hindi cinema, the character type has found an echo in films like *Tarana* (1951), *Guddi*, *Khubsoorat* and *Jab We Met*

---

20 Ibid.

(2007) in roles played by Madhubala, Jaya (Bachchan neé Bhaduri), Rekha and Kareena Kapoor respectively.

Except that there are elements to all the characters mentioned above that actually defy the simplistic boundaries that the term Manic Pixie Dream Girl seeks to impose on them. Indeed, Rabin himself lamented recently that the ubiquity of the term has led to lazy, convenient dismissals of women's parts that, when studied closely, are far more complex than the label allows.[21] And certainly describing, say, Annie Hall as nothing but a regressive male fantasy, or Guddi as having no interior life, would not only be disingenuous but completely and glaringly incorrect.

Based on a first glance, it is tempting to confine *Ijaazat*'s Maya to that familiar, reductive rubric. She is childlike in her effervescence, infectiously excited about the tiniest of things (such as learning how to ride a motorcycle), impulsive in a manner that denotes an insatiable hunger for all of life's pleasures and her rather unremarkable man appears to be the centre of her universe. As embodied by Anuradha Patel, she is also almost preternaturally ethereal.

Patel was a relative newcomer at the time she was cast in *Ijaazat* but she was certainly no stranger to the film world.

---

21 Nathan Rabin, 'I'm sorry for coining the phrase Manic Pixie Dream Girl', *Salon*, 16 July 2014, https://www.salon.com/2014/07/15/im_sorry_for_coining_the_phrase_manic_pixie_dream_girl/, accessed on 29 November 2018.

Her mother, Bharati Jaffery, was the eldest daughter of the Hindi film icon Ashok Kumar, affectionately called Dadamoni by friends and industry insiders, and her uncle was the legendary playback singer Kishore Kumar. Patel grew up on the periphery of the limelight that comes with being a movie star. 'I was often with my grandfather,' she recounts. 'I saw a very humble side of him. I noticed how motivated he was with work; I remember going to his shoots. People would go into a frenzy at the sight of him! He enjoyed it all and joked with everyone.'

Patel's most notable film role up to that point had been in Girish Karnad's *Utsav* (1984), for which she had received positive notices, and her familial background also helped in making her a familiar face amongst young film hopefuls, ensuring that *Ijaazat* fell into her lap with ease. 'In contrast to the character of Sudha, Maya had to have a younger vibe,' says Gulzar. 'I knew Anuradha from before, she being Dadamoni's granddaughter, and I had met her a number of times. She had Maya's girlishness; in fact, she has it to this day! Some traits remain no matter how old you get.'

Patel recalls: 'Originally, the film was to be made with Sanjeev Kumar, Hema Malini and Rekha. But it didn't happen. I think Gulzar bhai couldn't find a producer at that time or something like that. Years passed, Sanjeev Kumar passed away and, when the film was revived, it was recast. I remember we were sitting at Gulzar bhai's place and he was narrating the story to Naseer, Rekha and me.

Rekha wanted to play Maya but Gulzar bhai had cast her as Sudha and said that no, Anuradha will play Maya.

'I had a very smooth experience on the shoot. I had worked with Ashok Mehta before on *Utsav* and Gulzar bhai, of course, is such an easy person to get along and work with. Throughout the shooting, he guided me beautifully. He told me that the one thing I didn't have to do was cry, which was a relief! I felt very close to the character and to the things she did, like writing on her lover's back or wanting a baby. I would think to myself, that's so me! Gulzar bhai allowed me to improvise the way I said the dialogues and my gestures. During the shooting of '*Mera kuch saaman*', he told me he was pleasantly surprised that I was enacting it with ease. I told him the expressions and gestures were just coming to me naturally. But there were a few things I couldn't do, like riding the motorbike! I tried, and Naseer even tried to teach me, but I gave up and told them I just couldn't do it. So they had to fake those shots, with me and the bike on a trolley. On the whole, though, I really identified with Maya, her way of thinking, her spontaneity; that free spirit is very much a part of me too.'

Again, it's all too convenient to categorize Maya as a cookie-cutter filmi sprite whose *raison d'être* is being an empty vessel for Mahendra's hopes and dreams to be nurtured in or, to paraphrase Virginia Woolf, a looking glass with the magic and power of reflecting the figure of man at twice its natural size. A closer look at how the character is placed within the screenplay, however, as well as the details she is etched with belies this rudimentary reading. To begin with, we hear about but do not see Maya until almost an hour into the film. Where the same device helps give Harry Lime an air of mystery in *The Third Man* (1949) and Gabbar Singh an aura of chilling menace in *Sholay*, in *Ijaazat* it suggests that, like her name implies, Maya is elusive, ephemeral. '*Dhoondne se nahi milegi woh*' (You won't find her by searching for her), Mona cautions Mahendra. Quite contrary to the comfort offered by the average always available and reliable dream girl, Maya as the fantasy woman is more complicated and challenging (though not an albatross around the neck in the vein of, say, Kavita Sanyal in Mahesh Bhatt's 1982 quasi-autobiographical *Arth*). She may love Mahendra but she feels the need to remind him periodically that he can't take her presence for granted, that she is not indentured to the demands of his whims or his lifestyle. Indeed, we first encounter Maya through a note she has left on a mirror for Mahendra, while she herself has pulled off one of her usual disappearing acts. Scribbled with lipstick, it says: '*Bina bataye chalay jaate ho, jaa ke bataoon kaisa lagta hai?*' ('You go away without telling me. Shall I go and show you how it feels?').

This initial brush with Maya through her writing in such an impermanent medium, and on a surface that is an inverted reflection of what is real, is significant for a number of reasons. It not only serves to reiterate the impulsive, mercurial aspect of Maya's personality but also underlines the illusory aspects of their relationship (or any romantic relationship, for that matter). Maya and Mahendra maybe 'a couple' but, for the former, that comes with the implicit expectation of adherence to the unwritten rule-book of romance, which is largely a one-way street of accountability and dependence favouring the man; something she clearly doesn't wish to be held to.

In this context, Maya's missive on the mirror also denotes an urge to break from the traditional literary and cinematic trope of the Waiting Woman. From fairytale to epic to novel to poetry to film, scores of women characters have been assigned the passive act of waiting as their primary role: waiting for love, waiting to be rescued, waiting for a husband/lover to return from his adventures or even just waiting for death, usually in the wake of romantic failure or absence. While faithful Penelope waits for Odysseus' return from his famous voyage, Sleeping Beauty takes a century-long nap awaiting true love's kiss (or sexual assault, depending on which version you read) to kick-start her life, which, of course, ends moments later with 'they lived happily ever after'. In Hindi films, the act of waiting is beatified repeatedly through song, from '*Aa intezar hai tera*' to '*Aayega aane wala*' to '*Aaja re pardesi*'. Thus, Maya's '*jaa ke bataoon kaisa lagta hai?*' is like a wry throwing down of the gauntlet to those fictional princes so used to coming home to a patient princess in the tower.

The idea is further cemented in another of Maya's poems, read out by Mahendra:

Chalte chalte mera saaya
kabhi kabhi yun karta hai
Zameen se utth ke
saamne aa kar
haath pakad kar kehta hai
Ab ki baar main aage aage chalta hun
aur tu mera peecha karke
dekh zara kya hota hai

(Sometimes, walking along,
my shadow leaves the ground,
stands facing me,
takes my hand and says
this time I'll walk ahead,
and you follow behind.
Let's see what transpires)

Gulzar is very fond of the lines: 'It's a very delicate poem, a very delicate idea, and it relates to the character, to her situation. I've thought about including that in my poetry collections many times.' It certainly is a poetically potent way for the character to assert her existence beyond that of her lover. Maya is not content to be a shadow, a form with no physicality, always following behind, always secondary, always subjugated. Again, love for her isn't about submission but about participation. She longs to be more than a passive fantasy, especially because, as we are shown, the fantasy is a fragile one already; one that breaks when reality hits too close. '*Ek bohot lambi saans mujhe udhaar de do na*, please, Poona *se* Mohenjodaro *tak*,' ('lend me a long, deep breath, won't you, from Poona to Mohenjodaro') she says to Mahendra over the phone, speaking to him for the first time since his wedding. Her own breath feels short, insufficient, to cope with her pain. Later, when she overhears Sudha's angry response to the idea of Maya coming to meet her, she is shattered. It is not hard to discern that her dejection arises not just from her separation from Mahendra but also from the realization that there cannot, realistically or practically, be a space for her in this marriage. And perhaps more than just Mahendra, what Maya truly desires is to have a sense of belonging, a soft place to fall. Whenever she refers to Sudha, she calls her 'didi' and often speaks of her in sensuous tones. '*Jaante ho*,' she tells Mahendra. '*Didi ki awaaz tumse pyaari hai, maano kaanch ke gale se nikal rahi hai*' (You know, didi's voice is sweeter than yours, as if she's made of glass). Perhaps she senses (or hopes for) in Sudha, more than in Mahendra, the stability and comfort of a family, maybe even a mother figure – both things that she has never had. Sudha's rejection and the ensuing argument between her and Mahendra also reconfirms for Maya her suspicion that the marital institution is inherently weak, no matter the individuals involved ('*Harr jagah wohi* ...' [it's the same everywhere]).

In one of the few moments Maya allows herself an expression of bitterness, she likens a crumbling marriage to a festering wound: '*Maine [shaadi] dekhi hai. [Rishte] khatam ho jaate hain, toot jaate hain. Lekin shaadi jab khatam hoti hai na, to sadne lagti hai*' ('I've seen marriages. When a relationship ends, it breaks. But when a marriage ends, it starts to rot'). It is an indirect reference to the failed union of her own parents, which left her in the care of an absent father and a negligent stepmother, who also eventually grew apart. Her scars seem to come as much from the loneliness of an indifferent upbringing as from being witness to anger and recrimination replacing love and trust in a marriage. Her matter-of-fact attitude towards her wounds masks how deep they go. 'I think the most beautiful part of the role was that it wasn't melodramatic,' says Patel. 'And the part of her that doesn't want to be committed, wants freedom, was very intriguing. It linked to her past, her background in which her parents didn't get along, so her reasons were understandable. There's a very important message there of how the foundation of love is laid at home for one's children; parents set an example for their children as to how to live their lives and what their expectations in love should be. Maya's parents were the cause of her fear of commitment, but also formed her strong sense of self-worth.'

The iteration of that self-worth through her poetry is thus doubly significant in that, while the content is indicative of her rejection of female passivity, the very act of writing is itself a statement of creative aspiration and an interior life in which emotion and intellect converse with each other to find external expression (one can conjecture as to whether there is an echo of Meena Kumari in Maya). 'I established early on in the film that Maya writes poetry; that is why "*Mera kuch saaman*" doesn't feel like it comes out of nowhere,' says Gulzar. 'The character had to have that consistency. Her poetry couldn't be a one-off anomaly. If she writes "*Mera kuch saaman*" later, then we need to see that she can write like that at other points too; that it's part of who she is. And that's also why she gets away with her idiosyncrasies and all that she does; it's an extension of her poetic licence. For her, simply rhyming couplets is not enough. There is poeticism in her behaviour as well. A poet can do that! When she tries to commit suicide and fails, she laughs about it because she took too many pills and, instead of dying, she threw up! These are the unique elements of that character.'

Eventually, Maya does die, as many of cinema's free spirits are wont to do because the universe, it seems, cannot bear the weight of their lightness. The sequence depicting her death is notable for a number of reasons. First, it's significant that she is killed in an accident involving a motorcycle, a vehicle that had earlier been employed as a marker of her rebellious streak (she doesn't ride side-saddle demurely behind a man but drives it herself, with the man clinging on for life in the backseat). Second, the motorcycle in this case doesn't crash; Maya is killed when her long scarf gets caught in the back wheel of the bike, breaking her neck. 'Maya was really just an innocent girl, very straightforward,' says Gulzar. 'With her, what you saw was what you got, which in its own way is quite extraordinary. Her end had to be out of the ordinary too. So, I incorporated the incident of how Isadora Duncan died when her scarf got caught in the wheel of her car. Maya is killed when her scarf becomes entangled in the wheel of the motorcycle. I think it went with the character and the scarf was established much earlier in the script, when Sudha finds it in the house and comments on how long it is.'

It's not difficult to see why a veiled homage to American dancer Isadora Duncan would be appealing to the director. Duncan, a pioneering and often controversial figure in the world of modern dance at the turn of the twentieth century, flouted traditional mores and morality in both her professional and private life. Where, as a dancer, she broke with the rigid teachings of classical ballet and invited scandal by often performing barefoot in public, she was openly bisexual in her personal life, had children out of wedlock and also declared herself a Communist. 'Some people said I had copied the idea of Maya's death,' Gulzar recalls wryly. 'Now I can comprehend the idea of copying from a fictional source, like a novel, but how does one "copy" from real life? It's a well-known historical fact that Napoleon used to often sleep on his horse. Now, if I have a character who does the same, it's taking inspiration from someone's life, not plagiarizing someone's work. There's a difference.' And what is Maya if not Duncan-esque, at least in spirit, to the extent which her cultural context allows? She even tries to assuage her maternal longings by bringing home a random baby, much to Mahendra's horror; which she can't comprehend because, for her, the heart should have what the heart desires. Though, when he suggests playfully that if she wants a child of her own they must get married, she is dismissive: '*Ek bacchay ke liye dus aur jhamelay saath khareedo*' ('Take on ten other problems for one child'). Clearly, her own experience with familial trappings has left her wary, even if she isn't immune to the charms of conventional romance and motherhood.

Perhaps most importantly, though, Maya's death occurs when Mahendra, intentionally or otherwise, tries to assert his male authority over Maya by putting her in her female place (of subjugation), so to speak. Additionally, he does so through words shocking in their violence – '*Gala ghont doonga!*' (I'll strangle you!) – threatening her because she wants to go find Sudha for him (his words have a terrible resonance at the moment of her death, of course). That, it turns out, is the deal breaker. 'Both Maya and Sudha valued themselves,' Patel opines. 'They both walked out on the man they loved because they felt devalued. Maya had a lot of self-respect. She did not stand for how Mahendra belittled her, even if in frustration, and she walked out. That verbal violence shattered her. I don't think she wanted to die, necessarily, it just happened.' (*Jaa ke bataoon kaisa lagta hai?*)

'Maya obviously isn't a typical Hindi movie "other woman"', writes Saibal Chatterjee. 'She isn't a vixen out to break a home. She only wants to live life to the hilt and on her own terms. For her, a relationship is about shared spaces and moments, not socially imposed bondages.'[22] Just as Sudha is bound by the traditions of conventional Indian womanhood, Maya is bound by her own notions of freedom and individuality. She may yearn for stability and emotional fulfilment, but not at the risk of losing her sense of self.

Patel identifies most strongly with Maya, for obvious reasons, but has sympathy for all three characters. 'Maya and Sudha are both compassionate but neither can handle the situation of being pulled in two different directions. So Mahendra is left alone, partly because he can't make up his mind and commit to one woman. But even that, I feel, was understandable. He couldn't just abandon Maya; he loved her after all, even though, as a married man, keeping in contact with her would be considered socially unacceptable. But he doesn't want to give up Sudha either.

---

22 Chatterjee, *Echoes & Eloquences*, p. 202.

'The three individuals were good people, but they couldn't connect with each other. They weren't black or white; they belonged in the grey areas. Nobody's a villain and nobody wants to hurt the other person, but they end up hurting each other anyway. I mean, even though Maya seems like the "other woman", she doesn't want to interfere in the marriage and tries very hard not to. Later in the story, she comes to live with Mahendra in order to look after him and does so without being married to him. This was against socially acceptable norms, but she was beyond all those considerations. She doesn't believe in the papers that sanction the legitimacy of relationships; she believes in emotional connections. I'm like that too. I believe in love and affection, not in a piece of paper.

'I truly believe *Ijaazat* was a film ahead of its time. I met the distributor's wife somewhere a few years ago and she told me that when *Ijaazat* was first released, they went into a loss but they've made so much money off it in the years since because people appreciated it much more later. DVD and CD sales have always been strong and the film is always playing on TV. I think that's wonderful and I wish more films like that could be made; that are so sensitively written and made. The complexities of the relationships in *Ijaazat* were handled so beautifully.'

And as for her director and how he felt about her performance, his disappointment at her losing out on the Filmfare Award for Best Supporting Actress speaks to

Gulzar's deep appreciation of what Patel brought to the part of Maya: 'She was sitting with her husband Kanwaljit next to my table. The moment the award went to Sonu Walia (for *Khoon Bhari Maang* [1988]), I saw her face fall. We were all expecting her to get it. That's one grouse I'll always have against Filmfare. I still feel bad about it.'[23]

---

23 Razdan, 'Gulzar on Ijaazat?'

chapter five

Teri Do Nigahon Ke Sahare

Mahendra

ॐ

On the subject of male actors, Gulzar is clear on who his preferences had been in the most pivotal part of his career as a director. 'Sanjeev Kumar, of course, had been the one person I could depend on anytime for anything,' he affirms. 'Sanjeev and [music director R.D. Burman] were my two eternal anchors. Very rarely did I work with someone else. Sanjeev even used to say to me, "Why do you ever cast anyone else besides me? Forget about Jeetu and all, your pictures won't run without me!" Such was his faith in me that he would never ask me to narrate the initial story to him; he knew he'd get a completed script and narration later. Whenever I approached him for a film, he'd just say, "*Haan, kar lo*" (Yes, let's do it). It was an honour for me and I feel indebted to him to this day. After Sanjeev Kumar,

Naseer is the one in whom I saw a true "actor". He could portray the arrogance of Ghalib, as well as the relative timidity of Mahendra in *Ijaazat*. I still believe that if I were to do *Devdas*, he would be the most suitable person for it. I see it in him.'

Ijaazat, too, was originally supposed to have Sanjeev Kumar in the lead role, but the actor had to opt out due to the worsening heart condition that would eventually take his life at the age of forty-seven. Gulzar told his producer that the only actor he would even consider as a replacement was Naseeruddin Shah. On his experience with the actor, he says: 'I think I know Naseer, the actor, better than many others and, in some respects, better than he knows himself because there are certain elements of yourself that even you yourself cannot identify and fathom. To tell you about how I feel about Naseer as an actor, I will digress a little [from *Ijaazat*], to when I cast him in *Mirza Ghalib* (Doordarshan – 1988).

'No one – not producer Jai Singh, not cameraman Manmohan Singh, not the assistants, not a single person on the whole unit – was in favour of taking Naseer as Ghalib. Not one. They were all imagining Ghalib as some kind of 'hero', some impossibly handsome, imposing figure. Farooq Sheikh's was the only other name which was mentioned that was remotely close to what I had in mind. Otherwise everyone was coaxing me to cast this big star, that big star, etc. I was bent upon taking Naseer because, somewhere in my head, it had clicked already. But nobody was willing to pay the remuneration Naseer was asking for. The money people would periodically land up at his place to try to negotiate a lower fee. One day, Naseer came to see me at my office. He asked me, firstly, to stop these so-and-so's from going to haggle with him – you can imagine the term he actually used! Then he said to me, "Gulzar bhai, when I was studying at St. Stephen's College many years ago, I wrote you a letter when I heard you were going to make a film on Ghalib [with Sanjeev Kumar]. In it, I asked you to wait till I had entered the industry and was old enough for the role; and not to make it with Sanjeev! Then I forgot about it. I entered films, made a place for myself and now that Ghalib is finally happening, do you really think I'll let anyone else play the part? No, not only will no one else play this part but me, I will also not accept even one *dhela* (cent) less than my asking price, so they can forget about it. Now let's have some tea." And I just smiled. That's the first instance I truly saw a glimpse of Ghalib in him; that ego, that arrogance, those were major elements of Mirza Ghalib. It's like the quality I saw in Dharmendra when I first cast him. Even if you meet him today, he's like a sweet, adolescent boy.

'When I conveyed my final decision of casting Naseer to the producer, and that too at his quoted price, he was in a fix. The project had already been passed by Doordarshan; everything was in place and ready for production to commence. He said to me that we won't be able to sell the project to advertisers. "But I thought we'd already worked that out with the agency," I said. He retorted that the agency was on board with Ghalib, not Naseer. So I said, "Alright, I'll tell you what: don't pay me for writing, don't pay me for directing, I'll do it for free. But I'll pay Naseer his price and do the project only with him." I said, "You can check your budget. You'll be in profit." He was perplexed but finally agreed, saying that whatever is made upon the first broadcast is what they'll keep; beyond that, it and whatever it makes belongs to me. As a result, till date, the rights of Ghalib remain with me. They weren't convinced about the saleability of the music either, not even Jagjit [Singh] himself! They first refused to let me shoot it on film, then they refused to even shoot it on high-bend. The entire series was eventually shot on low-bend; they had so little faith in it.'

The outcome of this dogged, almost preternatural confidence that Gulzar placed in his actor need hardly be recounted: even today, thirty years after it first aired, *Mirza Ghalib* is considered a benchmark in South Asian broadcasting history and a career zenith for both Shah and the director.

Revered thespian, leading light of 'art' cinema, sellout, enfant terrible – Naseeruddin Shah has been bestowed with many titles during his long journey from being billed as 'standing behind dead doctor' in Rajendra Kumar starrer

Aman in 1967 and making his first splash in the Hindi parallel cinema movement with Shyam Benegal's *Nishant* (1975), to his current status as Indian theatre and film's straight-talking elder statesman. He has a well-deserved reputation as one who doesn't suffer fools gladly, and yet is always open to working with younger, inexperienced filmmakers. 'I don't go by whether someone is making a film for the first time,' he says. 'It's a throw of the dice in any case. I go by whether I feel like doing the project, the script, the reasons for the film to be made, the circumstances it's being made in and the kind of people who're making it.' It's this adventurous spirit that, one imagines, has ensured that he not only remains consistently in demand as an actor but that his body of work also is an enviably varied one. Connoisseurs of 'serious' films admire him for *Sparsh* (1980), *Paar* (1984), *Albert Pinto Ko Gussa Kyun Aata Hai* and the like; hard-core masala fans love him for movies like *Jalwa* (1987), *Tridev* (1989) and *The Dirty Picture* (2011); and middle-cinema enthusiasts cite *Masoom* (1983), *Jaane Bhi Do Yaaro* (1983), *Mirch Masala* (1987), etc., as their favourite Naseeruddin Shah films. *Mirza Ghalib* fans are a category unto themselves. And then, of course, there is *Ijaazat*.

'*Libaas* (1988 – unreleased in India) had been my first experience working with Gulzar bhai and I was delighted that he asked me to act in his film because I loved his work,' Shah recalls. 'It was a lovely film and we really enjoyed making it. Shabana [Azmi] was at her peak; Raj Babbar also did a good job in it. It had a lot to do with Gulzar bhai's guidance and I immediately found, to my great joy, that he and I had a tremendous tuning. We understood each other. He didn't even have to explain the character to me; I could see what needed to be done where. In fact, I think he had to give the least amount of direction to me. Shabana had a tougher part, and a very interesting one, of this lonely woman who at one point rekindles her relationship with her ex-lover, played by Babbar. Gulzar bhai was happy with my work and shared that with many people. Unfortunately, there was some issue with the producer and so *Libaas* never got released.

'In the years after, I kept hoping that he'd come to me with *Ghalib*, which he had planned off and on, sometimes with Sanjeev Kumar, then with Mr Bachchan, etc. Instead, he came to me with *Ijaazat* and, again, it was enough that he wanted me in his movie. I agreed to do it without even knowing much about the script. I would've done any part in it; it just so happened that he wanted me for the lead.

'Not many people know that before Gulzar bhai, Mrinal Sen wanted to make this story and he wanted to make it in real time, which was an idea that really thrilled me. But somehow, I think he was never able to write a script which could encompass two hours of real time action, and that too without going into flashbacks. Eventually, he abandoned the idea. So, when Gulzar bhai took it up, I was delighted. He, of course, gave it his own take. If Mrinal*da* had made it, it would've been a very different film and not half as successful, I suspect, because he was not a romantic at all but a hard-nosed realist. I don't even know what sort of angle he might have given it; he probably would've made the male lead an activist or something!

'I have to say the story of *Ijaazat* didn't much catch my fancy when I first heard it. It seemed somewhat regressive. The "sanctity of marriage" aspect, which there's nothing wrong with at the same time; it just depends on how you look at the world. But I still went happily into it. It was a high-profile film and I was starring opposite Rekha, who was also at the peak of her popularity. The other thing that drew me to the project, apart from the idea of working with Gulzar bhai again, was that I had never played a character in love before. For some reason, I'd never get cast in such characters and I'm also kind of happy about that because the way that they portray people falling in love in the majority of our movies is downright stupid and I don't think I'd ever be able to pull it off. And, of course, if you notice, the process of falling in love is always skimmed over. It just "happens", and that too in a day! Whereas *Ijaazat* did tackle the process of a marriage falling apart and another relationship developing. I thought it did that quite well.'

It's interesting that Gulzar mentions *Devdas* as a possible vehicle for Shah, considering that *Ijaazat*'s Mahendra bears something of a resemblance to Sarat Chandra Chattopadhyay's beloved romantic loser – minus the rampant alcoholism and penchant for self-destruction, that is. There is even a moment in the film that points to this analogous connection: Mahendra returns to the waiting room, having gone to find food for Sudha and himself, and upon finding the door locked from the inside, raps on the glass segment and calls out, 'Devdas! *Darwaza kholo* (open the door), Chandramukhi!' (It's also fitting he calls Sudha by the name of the woman who gave Devdas her heart but couldn't quite win his).

Other than the fact that both stories feature unconventional love triangles, which was the most obvious connect, the male protagonists who form the fulcrum of these triangles are both interesting but rather unremarkable men who, inexplicably, attract the love of two beautiful, passionate and fiery women. Mahendra – Maha Indra – is the centre of Sudha and Maya's concentric universes; is he really worthy of their devotion or are the women selling themselves short for the love of an altogether undeserving man? (Not that they'd be the first women in the history of romantic love to do that). The film does not dwell directly on this question, and perhaps we aren't meant to either, but there is enough evidence to suggest that, like Devdas, Mahendra is the architect of his own despair because he lacks the fortitude to face the vagaries of love and circumstance. Where Devdas seeks refuge in the form of self-flagellation from the fact of his own impotence in the face of socio-familial pressures, Mahendra remains a perpetual bystander in his own life's narrative, contributing only weakly, grudgingly even, to the course it will take.

In keeping with his reimagining of the original text, Gulzar also tinkered with details of the character. 'I changed Mahendra's profession to that of a photographer from an employee at some firm,' he says, 'and with it came that associated "rebellious" lifestyle.' Lifestyle is an apt word here because it denotes a certain frivolousness; a façade of a particular identity rather than a commitment to it. Certainly, Mahendra carries the required accoutrements of a constructed persona but those repeatedly prove feeble in the fight for dominance when faced with the pull of his roots. For, as we are shown, Mahendra is not born to the city manor but as the scion of a traditional, Brahmin, land-owning family based in an unnamed village. The benevolent patronage of his grandfather, though, has allowed him to dodge the expectations that come with being who he is: to follow the norms of traditional and familial malehood to ultimately become a cog in the feudal structure. Instead, Mahendra fulfils his ambition to become part of a 'modern' urban middle class. Armed with a camera instead of a scythe, riding a motorbike in place of a bullock cart, wearing denim instead of a dhoti, he seeks to position himself in the India of the future, not the past. In fact, he goes a step further than gaining simple urban affluence and assertion of independence; his aspiration includes acquiring bohemian credentials, as symbolized by the free-spirited Maya. In this light, one has to wonder if Mahendra's choice of romantic partner didn't have a certain cynical (even subconsciously so) calculation behind it; that is, if it was his choice to begin with. Through what we can discern about his personality, it's not hard to imagine that, in this liaison, Maya was the pursuer and Mahendra the pursued. After all, the latter, as a character, is marked by a glaring, dogged passivity that is at the heart of the inertial love triangle formed around him. He waits for things to happen or for others to make them happen.

Mahendra's chronic inaction, even in the face of life-changing situations, is a running motif throughout the film. Despite living with Maya for years, he has never told anyone in his household about her; it most certainly must be part of his consideration that such an arrangement would be more than frowned upon, not to mention that he has already been promised to Sudha. Even when he is cornered, Dadu having informed him that his overdue wedding to Sudha is soon on the cards, his response is to turn to his wife-to-be for a solution. (He will, in fact, constantly look to her for answers to dilemmas of his own making.) Revealingly, he states that he had secretly been hoping that she would have found someone else by now, presumably so that he wouldn't have to break the engagement and expose the truth of his love affair and, more importantly, so that he didn't have to be answerable. Even at this juncture, Sudha tells him to have faith in

Dadu and come clean to him, assuring him that the older man will not force him to do anything against his will. But Mahendra can't bring himself to do so; not at this point and not when Maya fails to reappear before the date of the wedding. Later, this same compulsive refusal to take responsibility for difficult decisions leads to Maya's undefined but troubling presence in the marriage, as well as Sudha's ultimate exit from it. Interestingly, his inability or unwillingness to confront potential adversity in his relationships is indicative not only of Mahendra's essentially passive nature but also of the notion that his escape from the norms and demands of his traditional background is merely physical and not a psychological one. In truth, he is only a rebel in secret. He may defy traditions but only when the safety of the distance between city and village provides a space for this masquerade of his 'unconventional' lifestyle to be played. Even there, he feels the weight of his accountability: in preparation for Dadu's visit, he unquestioningly puts on the *janeyu* (sacred thread), though he never wears one otherwise; his constant acquiescence in familial and romantic transactions carries a mix of guilt, respect, fear and a near-cynical instinct for self-preservation. If you lay low and still enough, you can't be blamed for the chaos you have wrought. In this context, it is ironic that Sudha seeks his permission to leave at the end, since his consistent passivity was, by default, a tacit approval for her to remove herself from the situation.

More ironic still, Sudha did find someone else to replace him in her life this time.

Mahendra is often a maddening character to contend with and might have been easily dismissed as being too self-involved to be relatable or sympathetic were it not for the hints of a resignedly melancholic self-awareness that he periodically displays. He is not oblivious to his failings but lacks the fibre to rectify them, and it is this very basic human weakness that Gulzar has sympathy for. 'There's a very telling argument between Sudha and Mahendra,' he says, 'when the latter says exasperatedly, "Sacrifice! Sacrifice! All the time sacrifice!" He's taunting her but he's also suffered because of it; because of her sacrificial nature. He's always felt so much smaller in comparison. By taunting her, he's hurting himself too.' It is also notable that what Mahendra refers to as a sacrifice is Sudha's assertion that he doesn't need to go searching for food outside the platform because she isn't hungry. That the issue of food is a weighty, symbolic reminder of all else Sudha has given up is lost on neither Mahendra nor the audience. It's an interesting paradox, and a believable one, that he is as resentful of her magnanimity as he is grateful for it because his selfishness is magnified by her largesse. His shame at his own inertia may also be compounded by the underlying realization that in the world he is from, his inaction puts a question mark over his role as an active member of a male-dominated milieu.

As Carol Pearson and Katherine Pope state in *Who am I This Time?: Female Portraits in British and American Literature*: 'Patriarchal society views women essentially as supporting characters in the drama of life; men change the world and women help them.'[24] Mahendra, though, appears helpless to change or to be in charge of his world, relying on the women in it to be its sculptors. As such, the issue of conventional masculinity might not be the crux of Mahendra's character but it is a part of it, certainly in the instances where he tries to assert his maleness through an aggressive, violent voice with both Sudha and Maya. In the absence of the other social trappings of his gender, this voice seems to be Mahendra's only active, though futile, attempt at claiming his place in a masculine world.

The act of referring to a trifle as a sacrifice rather than, say, a compromise may also be a wry way of the writer to further underline Mahendra's tendency towards an everyday fatalism that seems to have settled into his latter-day persona. For the Mahendra of the waiting room, his past (and, one suspects, his awareness of his own role in it) has taken a toll: small inconveniences appear to him as small calamities, which he greets with an exasperated, defeated 'Oh, hell!' From not finding a coolie, to the incessant rain,

---

24 Carol Pearson and Katherine Pope, *Who Am I This Time?: Female Portraits in British and American Literature*. New York: McGraw-Hill, 1976, pp. 4–5.

to a faulty light bulb in the waiting room toilet, Mahendra now sees insurmountable difficulties in life's trivialities. Fitting, perhaps, for a man who has lost everything of meaning and so has the luxury, maybe even a need, to make mountains out of molehills.

It is this tangle of foibles and frailties that ultimately makes Mahendra an intriguing study, particularly because he is deceptively one-dimensional at first glance. Gulzar's writing, coupled with Naseeruddin Shah's portrayal, etches out a character that is both complex and sympathetic. The audience can relate to an individual who is torn not only between two women but also two worlds; between his society and his individuality, between the demands of his gender role and his own 'flaws' of character. Mahendra may desire to be, and even believe himself to be, as 'free' as Maya appears to be but, in their own ways, they are both victims of tradition: she loses to it, he defers to it and both are poorer for it. He ends up (momentarily) with Maya, not because he gathers the courage to change his circumstances but because Sudha does – for all three of them. And it is the mark of a multi-layered character that we are left with questions whose answers lead us right back to his core. Why, for instance, does Mahendra not try to contact Sudha after Maya's death, even if it's just for closure and not reconciliation? Is he simply respecting her wishes or is it the familiar fear of having to face the outcome of his own doings? Gulzar leaves us to draw our own conclusions, or to not draw any at all: his characters are rich enough without having to be explained down to the last ambiguity.

For the actor playing the part, it was the rigours of the shoot more than the intricacies of the character that often proved to be a tougher deal. Naseeruddin Shah recalls: 'The shooting went on for so long that I must admit I kind of lost interest in it in places and I think that affected my performance. There were a few scenes that I just didn't find convincing enough to be able to play them with conviction, and it makes me cringe to think of how I performed them, but it was mainly the prolonged duration of the shoot that bothered me. I was unhappy about that and I got impatient because I felt it should've been quicker. I had grown a beard for the waiting room portions of the film, because I hate sticking fake beards, and we hoped to finish those parts in one go but that didn't happen. So, I ended up having to stick on a fake beard for some of the scenes. But it is those portions of the film that I love because the situation itself is so emotionally rich that it grabs you. And the twist at the end is fantastic.'

There are happier memories too, of course, particularly when it comes to remembering the many perks and advantages of working with someone like Gulzar. 'That little bit with the faulty bulb in the waiting room toilet was improvised and Ashok Mehta grumbled about it but we managed to convince him! And that's the great thing about Gulzar bhai; he's so open to suggestions but he knows exactly where to draw the line too. For some reason, he always insists that his lead male characters have moustaches, you won't see a Gulzar film where the male lead doesn't have a *moochh*! I grew my own beard and moustache for the waiting room scenes but I didn't want any facial hair for the flashbacks. Gulzar bhai insisted on a moustache and it was too late to grow one, so I had to stick a fake one on. And it looks stuck on! But he did not compromise on his image of the character.

'At the same time, though, he's also very open when he sees the point and if it makes sense to him. For example, when he first saw what I was planning to wear as the character, he told me, "No, no, that's not right." So I said to him that Gulzar bhai, this is what he would wear. He wouldn't wear a crumpled kurta all the time; that's Sudhir from *Libaas*, not Mahendra. This chap is a bit of a blade. He should be sharply dressed, wearing some cool stuff like denims and shirts. And he saw my point and agreed. He was the same way during *Ghalib*. I didn't know as much about the character as he did but whenever I hesitantly offered a suggestion, he would be open to it and often incorporated it.

'The way he constructs his scenes is also very rare. Other filmmakers will simply tell you, okay, you sit here, you sit there and I'll shoot you talking to each other. But I think Gulzar bhai and Shekhar Kapur are the only two directors I've worked with who say that they want to look at what a character is doing; and that is the approach that an actor must also have. Actors worry too much about what a character is feeling. They should worry about what the character is doing, because that is what's evoking the feeling. The way Gulzar bhai works out your actions on screen – half your work is done for you. And, of course, he writes such wonderful dialogue, and creates such great situations, that all you have to do really is personify the character. That's all I really did in his films and I get so much credit for it, which I happily accept because refusal of praise indicates a desire to be praised again! But I make it a point to acknowledge the fact that were it not for Gulzar bhai, I could not have done whatever I did. And that was also the case with my being able to play a character who was smitten with two women at the same time. He wasn't self-destructive like Devdas, though!'

Both as actor and audience, Shah has admired Gulzar's work for a long time: 'The great thing about Gulzar bhai's films is that he explored areas of life that commercial Hindi cinema didn't really touch upon and in a very original manner, I must say. His film *Parichay* had the most believable performances by children in a Hindi film of the popular genre. *Masoom* is the only other film that had convincing performances by children. His sensibility is just so different; and it's there right from his earliest films like *Achanak* and *Mere Apne*, which I loved. His films couldn't be boxed into a single category, and his style became a byword: 'Gulzar type' films. In fact, I think he extended the idiom of his gurus, Bimal Roy and Hrishikesh Mukherjee. He absorbed the right things from them and then took them further.'

He also laments that the idiom is no longer in vogue: 'Now there is no one who makes those kinds of movies. That entire genre of films has disappeared. Look at the monster filmmaking has become. Can you imagine anyone backing a film like *Ijaazat* today? It was not a small budget film by any means, even though Rekha was the only big star in it, but Gulzar bhai was able to get financial backing for it. Today the first thing they'd want to know is how much money it's going to recover. It would have to be made very cheaply and you couldn't have a big star like, say, Deepika Padukone with next to no money. So, nobody attempts those movies because, among the producer fraternity at least, all they're interested in is quick returns and not good cinema. People like Gulzar bhai have been put away on a shelf.'

Though Shah has never really counted *Ijaazat* among his personal favourites as an actor, passage of time seems to have mellowed his attitude towards it. 'I've had mixed feelings about *Ijaazat* since I made it,' he says candidly. 'I saw it only once when it was released. Of late I've started to think that I should watch it again and see how I feel about it now. So many people talk so fondly about it and they speak of it in the same breath as *Masoom, Sparsh, Jaane*

Bhi Do Yaaro and *Ghalib*. Something about it resonates with a lot of people. And it was, in every way, good for me because it was one of the few middle cinema movies being made at the time; the kind of movies that needed an actor like me. That was part of my calculation when I decided to go to the Film Institute after studying at drama school. I had seen films by Shyam Benegal, Basu Chatterjee and Hrishikesh Mukherjee, and I felt that sooner or later their kinds of films were going to need an actor like me. And that did happen; that's how I started in films.

'*Ijaazat* is also among those films because it's a part I think no star would have touched because he's a weak man; he's not heroic and, in fact, he's pretty despicable at times. But it was good for me as it introduced me to a whole new audience: Gulzar bhai's, which is a segment in itself; the people who would go and see every film of his and still to this day talk of films like *Angoor*, *Aandhi* and *Khushboo*.

'Eventually, *Ijaazat* also taught me a very important lesson: that the true soul of a filmmaker always shines through in any film that is made. It's always a reflection of oneself and, in many cases, an idealized version of oneself. Like the kind of films that Manmohan Desai, etc., made; the Bachchan persona was an idealized version of themselves. In Gulzar bhai's case, it's work of a different sensibility but one can easily see where it touches on the autobiographical.'

On the personal front, too, Shah speaks of his director in only the fondest of terms: 'One of the most memorable parts of making *Ijaazat* for me was during the location shoot at Mangalore when I taught him how to play tennis at the courts there. At that time, he was an avid badminton player; he used to play from five to eight in the morning every day. So, one day, I said to him, '*Aap* tennis *khel ke dekhiye*' (You should give tennis a try). And I converted him – now he plays tennis from five to eight! Otherwise, too, Gulzar bhai has a very healthy lifestyle: he rarely drinks, and only if he has company; he goes to bed early, wakes up early ... He's almost too sane! But it's great to be around him because he's such a balanced person. Sometimes, if I'm troubled, he's the guy I confide in as he's a very good listener. I just wish he didn't idealize his women so much!'

chapter six

Jhoot Moot Ke Shikve Kuch

Sudha

℃℞

'I've led many lifetimes in one, and I've explored myriad aspects of Indian womanhood.'

– Rekha

In its many visits to the story of a married man torn between two women, Hindi cinema has usually painted the role of the wife in the same broad strokes of silent suffering, unwavering faith and unconditional forgiveness. She will wait patiently, confident in her belief that her 'goodness', contrasted against the inherent 'badness' of the Other Woman, will make her erring husband realize the folly of his ways and he will return, chastised and grateful, to the folds of home, hearth and her sari. It is a cliché employed so thoughtlessly over the decades that it became a parody of itself – '*Bhala hai, bura hai, mera pati mera khuda hai*' (Good or bad, my husband is my god), sang one obliging *patni* as her husband cavorted with another.

But *Ijaazat*, as is abundantly clear in so many ways, does not play by the conventional Hindi film rule-book. If Maya is a world away from the stereotypical scheming, amoral Other Woman, and Mahendra much more than an 'unsympathetic ogre,'[25] Sudha, too, is not a cookie-cutter sacrificial lamb of a spouse whose floods of tears cynically paint crude columns of black and white in the morality stakes. Instead, in Sudha we find Gulzar's assertion that womanhood is neither easily defined nor streamlined into convenient categories that act as little more than reductive mirrors for men's egos to be magnified or, as the case may be, get a dressing down in. Sudha, like all of Gulzar's women, is an individual, not a cut-out, who possesses both an astounding self-awareness as well as the ability to read others better than they can read themselves. Not that she sees these qualities, or herself overall, as anything extraordinary: '*Main ek bohot saadharan aurat hun*' (I'm a very ordinary woman), she writes in her farewell letter to Mahendra. '*Ziddi bhi hun, jal bhi jaati hun, pighal bhi jaati hun*' (I'm stubborn, I burn easily, and I melt easily too). In defining her own weaknesses, though (and it's arguable whether they can be classified as such), Sudha inadvertently proves herself to be

---

25 Chatterjee, *Echoes & Eloquences*, p. 201.

anything but ordinary; a woman whose very transparency makes her a near-enigma. That she is played by Rekha is casting that is not only intelligent but also prescient in its understanding of an actor who, in the decades since, has come to be regarded as an intriguing amalgam of talent, presence, personality, persona and legend, and who, much like Sudha, has consistently defied simplistic categorization.

While the trajectory of Rekha's career has most often been described in the familiar terms of the ugly duckling turning into a beautiful swan, that cliché fails to acknowledge that that transformation, as well as her longevity in an industry well-known for its sexist attitudes, has been about much more than just looks. Her larger-than-life image, one that still inspires awe in fans both old and young, is not one carved out of frivolity but which carries with it the foundation of a woman of substance, who is acutely aware of the meaning of that image and also wise enough to be able to cast an objective, critical eye on herself as both actor and persona. 'In real life, I'm shy and introverted,' she admits. 'That's why I'm fiery on screen. The switching on of the camera is my "go" signal.'

A Telugu-speaking tomboy who was 'a big clown in school [...] but was never close to anybody, never had a best friend, [and a] black sheep because [she] was fat and ugly'[26],

---

26 Anil Saari, *Indian Cinema: The Faces Behind the Masks*, New Delhi: Oxford University Press, 2011, p. 100.

Bhanurekha Ganeshan joined Hindi films barely into her teens so that, as she candidly expressed, she 'wouldn't have to use her brains'. She overcame the language barrier quickly enough, thanks to having a good memory, and found herself attaining the tag of a sex symbol. 'At that age, you are so naïve that you don't know what is happening; you feel it's a feather in your cap,' said the actor. 'Then I began to realize that people were taking advantage of my innocence or my age and were trying to cash in on it.'[27] She went through various stages where she struggled with the 'sexy' image; sometimes fighting it, other times reconciling with it on her own terms, all the while wary that heroines who were deemed sexy were rarely regarded as good actors. Eventually, her growing confidence in the quality of her craft allowed her to embrace her onscreen sensuality: 'I think it is a plus point for me. [If] a woman is desirable and a good actress, then there's nothing quite like it. I'm very proud of having this quality. A beautiful woman does get used to being admired. It gives her a lot of confidence and, in my case, that confidence is sort of set inside me and it will remain inside me for life.'[28]

That confidence has often made Rekha less than circumspect in the appraisal of her own work. She was famously emphatic in her contention that she didn't deserve

---

27 Ibid., p. 106.
28 Ibid., p. 107.

the National Award for Best Actress for *Umrao Jaan* (she felt it should have gone to Jennifer Kendal for *36 Chowringhee Lane* [1981]): 'I looked beautiful but my performance was nothing. [And] I'm not being modest.'[29] But she is also refreshingly knowledgeable about her own personal process as a performer, confessing to becoming anxious as the first day of shooting approaches: 'An actor who is about to get under the skin of a new character is like a bride adopting a new family after an arranged marriage. You are under a microscope, judged by everyone on the set. It can be very unnerving!

'I have not studied acting and I have not done theatre, so there is no definite method for me. When I was new, I was indifferent to my work and didn't give a damn whether I got the scene right or wrong. Later, as I evolved, I didn't want to understand the method because it takes away the magic. Acting is more of a spontaneous reaction. Eventually, of course, the moment of truth for all actors is when the director calls "start camera". What happens prior to this happens at a subconscious level. It could be something I have watched from my car window and stored in my memory bank for years.'[30]

Rekha may not have a term to describe this method (or lack thereof) but the efficacy of it has meant that apart

---

29 Ibid., p. 81.
30 Somaaya, *Talking Cinema*, p. 81.

from being one of the most successful actors in commercial Hindi cinema, she has also been in demand with Mumbai's parallel and middle cinema filmmakers, from Shyam Benegal, Girish Karnad and Muzaffar Ali to Hrishikesh Mukherjee, Basu Bhattacharya and Govind Nihalani. Gulzar, too, saw elements in her that were right for the character for Sudha. 'Rekha is eternally a girl and yet, at the same time, has a maturity about her,' says the director. 'Again, it's there in her body language, in her voice. Let me recall to you the scene in which a waiter at the railway station, upon finding Mahendra's suitcase unattended, tries to snoop around in it and Sudha tells him off. That authority in her voice, the confidence with which she says it, says much more than a friendship; it's the relationship that's speaking. And then the way she closes the suitcase and walks back to her chair, that's a wife walking, not a girlfriend. I can't quite explain it but that's how it reads to me. It's the walk of a woman who holds the keys to the household in her *pallu*, not a girlfriend visiting that household. That's the kind of physicality Rekha brought to the part, which I knew she would. She has that confidence of a mature woman.'

It must have helped, of course, that Sudha is herself such a richly layered character to play. Contrary to the stereotypically submissive, self-pitying filmi wives, as well as her own assessment of herself as an ordinary woman, Sudha is, in fact, a complex and unpredictable individual. She may see herself as uncomplicated but her responses to her situation are anything but. '*Jal bhi jaati hun, pighal bhi jaati hun,*' she says; and certainly, the landscape of emotions she traverses in between these two apparent extremes is varied and nuanced. There is also the underlying proximity of the ideas of burning and melting implied by the two words '*jal*' and '*pighal*' which indicates that for Sudha, her own awareness of her moments of conventional jealousy ironically serve to make her feel even more deeply for Mahendra and Maya's vulnerabilities. 'Sudha is a married woman, I'm not,' says Rekha. 'But I understand her. She could see in plain view that Maya loves and, more importantly, needs Mahendra more than she does. She's that sensitive. I think she's the ideal woman, but not to others, not to everyone. Not everyone wants the "ideal" person.'

One of the most striking aspects of Sudha's unexpected complexity is expressed during a flashback early in the film, when Mahendra comes clean to her about Maya in the hopes that she will call off the wedding. Sudha's cool, calm, almost amused reaction to Mahendra's barely veiled confession of a live-in sexual relationship is surprising, not only because Mahendra is, for all intents and purposes, her fiancé but also because the audience probably expects a more morally offended, less level-headed, response from someone of Sudha's background. She is, after all, just a school teacher from a small town and Hindi cinema is not in the habit of defining such characters' world views in anything but the narrowest, most myopic terms. But Sudha is unfazed, indicating that though her upbringing may be strictly traditional, she is familiar with and understands modern mores; they may be out of her experience but she won't pass judgement on them either. At this juncture, she advises Mahendra to talk to Dadu; to do what is 'truthful and right'. We may wonder why she doesn't volunteer to advocate before Dadu on his behalf but it is important that she does not, perhaps because it's her way (and only the first instance of many) of pushing Mahendra to be a better man, to be righteous, to be truthful and to fight his own battles. As Gulzar puts it, 'What is right isn't always true and what is true isn't always right; and neither is it easy or convenient.' Yet Sudha is depicted as being in a constant struggle to achieve both, especially in the absence of a similar commitment from her husband. She may brew the tea and deal with the dhobi, but she's also the one who pushes for a resolution to the situation and finally makes the torturous decision to end the marriage. And it is at this point that she does speak to Dadu to defend Mahendra, asking him not to chastise his grandson. '*Main to bus nikal aayi hun, isse bahana keh lo ya kaaran keh lo*' (I've just left; you can call it an excuse or a reason), she says, her words echoing her resignation to the fact that Mahendra could not, ultimately, be the man she needed him to be. His love for another woman (and Sudha's sympathy for that) may not be an excuse for her walking out, but it's certainly not the whole reason either.

Sudha's patience in the face of Mahendra's weakness and indecision through the course of their marriage, then, is puzzling and even infuriating. More so because, as somewhat objective onlookers, we see that while she is a quietly remarkable woman, he is a man who has dressed up his ordinariness in the rags of urban bohemia. Sudha appears to be selling herself short for the love of a man who hardly seems to be worthy of the struggle she puts herself through. Mahendra's indulgent coddling for Maya is possibly an antidote to her own neuroses and fears of abandonment, but Sudha seems to simply be urging him to become the uncomplicated, conventional husband who embodies the simple traditions of where she comes from and finds comfort in. Perhaps we are meant to surmise that though Sudha herself is quite extraordinary, her needs and desires are not; perhaps it is the tranquility of mundane domesticity that she seeks.

This patience extends beyond Mahendra to Maya as well and, in fact, it is Sudha's relationship with the other woman that is even more intriguing than the one with her husband. From the outset, there is an 'invisible, barely articulated bonding that exists between the two women. They have never met each other and yet, somewhere deep down, they are able to understand each other's compulsions'.[31] Again, atypical of the 'wronged' filmi spouses, Sudha is more than

---

31 Chatterjee, *Echoes & Eloquences*, p. 202.

sensitive to Maya's emotions; on some plane, there is a recognition of the shared pain of womanhood that may take on different forms but whose effects are familiar to a woman shown to be empathetic to all those around her.

Rekha sees something even deeper in Sudha's tenderness towards Maya: 'A woman is born a woman and a mother, whether she physically bears a child or not. I feel the mother is more important [than the father], possibly because I've only known my own. And I think there is something motherly in what Sudha feels for Maya.' There is certainly something maternal in the way Sudha indirectly indulges Maya, like the way a parent is indulgent of a wilful but lovable child. '*Iss pagli par taras bhi aata hai, pyar bhi aata hai*' (I feel sorry for this silly girl, and affection too), she says, when Maya sends Mahendra a birthday rose. 'This delicate moment comes from the core of her being. It's not said for the sake of it, just to say an "impressive" line,' Gulzar asserts, 'because that is not the kind of thing one says casually in passing; it comes from within. And it says something very powerful about her and their relationship that she can say it.' That Sudha speaks of feeling affection and sympathy, but not anger, is notable because it is so very reminiscent of parental benignity and also reinforces the idea of her being a woman whose emotions are raw and unfettered from societal norms and expectations.

Her approach towards Maya is revelatory precisely because it is so far removed from the kind of sanctimonious territoriality we normally see from a character grappling with a third presence in their marriage. This generosity of spirit momentarily takes on almost surreal proportions when Sudha, cheerily and without missing a beat, appears to agree to Maya's request (expressed in a flashback) that Mahendra and his wife give her their hypothetical baby. Of course, this 'consent' is given jokingly and immediately retracted but what is significant about this moment is that Sudha's reaction is, again, not only sporting but also instinctually charitable; she could easily have chosen to treat the request seriously and taken offence. Instead, her response is exactly in the vein that we have come to recognize as being characteristic of her: kind and empathetic. There is also the underlying suggestion that Sudha identifies and understands Maya's need for being nurtured but also for being a nurturer better than Mahendra does, for he seems to put down this apparent whim of Maya's to mere childish compulsiveness while she can comprehend Maya's strong desire to be a mother as something legitimate – an adult desire – also indicated subtly in her retraction, for she herself desires the same.

Almost despite herself, Sudha does try to assert her more supposedly traditional 'female' self at various points by claiming a modicum of ownership over both her husband and their shared domestic space. And yet, in each instance, the largesse of her emotions overrides the streak of possessiveness her mind attempts to impose on her.

In the precursory scenes to '*Mera kuch saaman*', for example, when she suggests that Mahendra should return Maya's things because they appear valuable and are going to waste sitting unused in their house, there is a momentary hint of covetousness in the seemingly innocent proposition; are we really supposed to believe that her intentions are so unselfish? Even as she makes a perfectly reasonable case for returning the items, we wonder whether the underlying reason isn't that she secretly hopes to banish Maya's memories from her home by first ridding it of her corporeal traces. But then, in the very next moment, when Mahendra acquiesces and says that he'll send the things over with a servant, Sudha chastises him: '*Bura lage ga*' (It won't look nice). She insists that he take the things across himself. Once again, Sudha proves herself to be much bigger than the cynicism of those who would doubt her strength of character.

For Gulzar, this was a pivotal moment. 'The scene where Sudha finds Maya's belongings, including the long scarf, was very important because it tells us what kind of a person Sudha is,' he opines. 'She wants Maya to have them. When Mahendra says that he'll have them delivered to Maya through a servant, Sudha is adamant that he must deliver them himself, otherwise it would look bad, i.e., it would be insensitive to Maya's feelings. So, she's not only an intelligent, progressive person but she's also large-hearted and capable of feeling for the "other woman". I suppose that's why Mahendra relies on her to solve everything.' Rekha views this side of Sudha with sympathy and admiration but is also acutely aware that, on some level, it must damage her too. 'People like Sudha, those with such an open, honest, generous spirit,' she says, 'they flow like water but can burn themselves in the process.' Certainly, in the aftermath of sending her belongings, when Maya expresses her hurt and anguish through the poetry of '*Mera kuch saaman*', Sudha is overcome with guilt at her own lapse of judgement. As Mahendra reads out Maya's words, whose delicate beauty cannot mask the deep wounds they arise out of, Sudha sobs on his shoulder, contrition written on her face and in her voice: '*Maine kyun bhijwaya woh sab?*' she admonishes herself through her tears. '*Yun bhi to Maya din raat hamare saath reh rahi hai, saaman bhi reh jata to kya ho jata?*' (Why did I send her things back? She's with us all the time anyway, so what if we'd kept her things as well?) In a different milieu, with more conventional Hindi film trappings, this scenario would perhaps have come off as almost absurd but we understand and accept these emotions from Sudha as not only plausible but expected; and it is due, in large part, to the sensitivity with which Rekha plays this moment. When enunciating these lines, she strikes an intricate balance between empathy and remorse, making it completely believable that Sudha is articulating the agony of the collective feminine experience of alienation that social norms so often engender.

In fact, Sudha seems to be locked in an ongoing struggle to negotiate her way around Maya's fragility and

Mahendra's ambivalence, while holding on to her own sense of self (and self-respect). She may be unconventional in her approach towards her situation but she is still a woman who is psychologically bound by the traditions of where she comes from and experiences the emotions fomented by those traditions. Again, she may allow herself to empathize with Mahendra and Maya but she won't compromise on her feminine pride in the bargain. Gulzar was mindful of the need to express and explore both facets of her character in all their complexities in order to keep her from becoming one-dimensional. 'There is a sense of balance in Sudha that is created through the dialogues,' he says, citing the scene where Sudha finds Maya's picture in Mahendra's wallet and cannot stop herself from expressing her displeasure: '*Sab kuch hi bata hua lag raha hai iss ghar mein ... poora poora apna kuch bhi nahi lagta*' (Everything feels shared in this house ... nothing feels like it's entirely mine). Such instances are crucial, the director feels, to help assert the idea of Sudha being a nuanced, layered character rather than a cipher for some shallow notion of womanhood. 'After all, she is the wife,' he says, 'so a sense of possession is there. But it's the same wife who later on removes her jewellery from her jewellery box to make room for Maya's love letters to Mahendra.' Sudha tells him: '*Apne zevar nikaal kar aap ke daal diye hain*' (I've removed my jewellery to make space for yours), creating an achingly sublime moment that underscores the profound notion that the value one places in possessions is assigned, not intrinsic.

'She has moments of weakness and selfishness too,' Gulzar elaborates, 'and those are important for creating a contrast with her moments of calm and level-headedness. You have to see those ups and downs on her graph; it can't be a straight line with no variation. And when I think about such instances from the film, I think I can claim some credit for being a good writer!' Indeed, in a sharp divergence from all the scenes in which Sudha puts aside her pride and her own desires to accommodate those of others, there is the shock of the scene where she unequivocally rejects Mahendra's proposal of inviting Maya to the house, not caring that the latter can hear the harshness of her words over the phone. It's a powerful moment precisely because it defies the image of Sudha the film has organically constructed up to that point, only to shatter it as a potent reminder that her charity and fortitude stretch only to the periphery till which Maya remains as a dynamic but distant fantasy. The possibility of her becoming too real, of stepping into Sudha's carefully guarded inner world, signals the end of not only the latter's patience but also her tryst with Mahendra's manufactured sanctum in which the traditions they are both tethered to could be temporarily suspended in the face of their individual dilemmas.

Like Sudha herself, her act of walking out of her marriage is anything but uncomplicated; not only in the sense of it being a virtual taboo as per societal and religious norms but also because the decision to do so arises out of an intricate web of overlapping emotions. While the impetus is provided by her continually wounded pride, it is painfully clear that she also takes the step out of compassion for Maya as well as a mix of pity and resentment towards Mahendra. No wonder, then, that she avoids rationalizing or even discussing her decision in any detail – '*Main to bas nikal aayi hun*' – for doing so would entail confronting the truth of the one thing that her marriage did not lack: love.

'Beauty is in the imperfect; beauty is in seeking and not always finding,' Rekha has said elsewhere, and it is an observation that poetically describes the trajectory that Sudha creates for herself. Her salvation lies not in hankering for some domestic-fairytale style moral triumph over the other woman, but in her valediction. In her farewell letter to Mahendra, she writes:'*Jaan boojh kar ek bhool ki thi – aap se shaadi kar li*' (I made a mistake on purpose – I married you); and thus she reveals her cognition of the preordained futility of her hope of carving out the normalcy or the mundanity of a stable, uncomplicated marriage from the leftovers of an incomplete love affair. It is a startling confession of her own complicity whose profundity is intensified by the brief exchange that takes place with her old school principal:

Mrs Khariwala:'*Talaaq lene ki soch rahi ho?*'
(Are you thinking of taking a divorce?)

Sudha: '*Nahi, dene ki soch rahi hun.*'
(No, I'm thinking of giving him one.)

Once again, Sudha is the giver but this is as much a final instance of generosity as it is an act of atonement to herself for disregarding her own better judgment earlier. To the bitter end, she does not compel Mahendra to make the choice she needs him to – leave her or leave Maya – because she knows he is capable of doing neither, and does what is 'truthful and right' to set him and herself free even as it wounds her. The task is a painful but necessary one, for in that pain lies her redemption which enables her to not only forgive Mahendra but also allow herself to move on.

'Sudha may not have "gotten" Mahendra but in the process of losing him, she found herself,' Rekha muses, 'which is something far more valuable in my view. That she also ended up with a wonderful man is almost incidental.' It is intriguing that the actor views the denouement of the story as a fairly happy one for Sudha, especially considering the final image of the film: a freeze-frame reminiscent of the closing shot of Satyajit Ray's *Charulata* (1964), ambiguous in its framing of the characters' future. In the composition, Mahendra is left alone outside the waiting room, gazing into the distance at Sudha as she turns to look at him one last time while her husband walks ahead of her. It is a powerful moment, underlining Mahendra's sense of loss and despair, as well as the hold that he – or, at least, the memory of him and their past together – still has over Sudha. Rekha acknowledges the power of nostalgia the moment captures but asserts that for her character, her husband is 'the love of her life. He is the male version of Sudha's character: an ordinary man but loving, free of ego. Look at his calm reaction when he realizes who Mahendra is. He only smiles; there's no anger, no jealousy, because he understands.' For her last thoughts on how she views Sudha's adaption to her new life and partner, the actor offers up her mother's words of advice about romance and marriage: 'She said to me, "Find a man who loves you a tad more than you love him." And I believe she was right. There is balance to be found in that imbalance. Women love more powerfully and selflessly than men.'

The long and often difficult shoot itself was a mixed bag for Rekha. 'On one hand, it was a tough time in my personal life,' she states. 'On the other, while calamity can be very chaotic, it also teaches you the most beautiful lessons.'Thus, she feels she was able to incorporate some of the emotions she was experiencing into her performance. And, more than anything else, it was the opportunity to be directed by Gulzar that brought her joy. 'The director is the "mother" on the set,' she says, 'and that's him [Gulzar]. His aura is joyous and peaceful and he makes the effort to build relationships with his cast and crew, relationships of love and trust. I call him my Babuji. I consider him my soul-mate and he admires me, which is also a huge responsibility.'

Rekha credits the director's generosity for getting her through some of the more difficult sequences in the film. In the scene where Sudha has to help Mahendra drape the *janeyu* in anticipation of Dadu's arrival, for example, the actor was a nervous wreck. 'I didn't know the *gayatri mantra!*' she recalls. 'I thought, "I can't even speak Hindi; how will I speak Sanskrit?" I started to cry because the shot was ready but I was not. Babuji calmed me down and wrote the words down for me in Roman. We took the shot and, in the film, you can't even tell that I had no idea what I was saying.' The actor enjoyed playing the simpler moments as much as the more dramatic ones, such as the scenes where she performs her domestic chores. 'I loved doing the housewifely things I never get to do in my own life,' she remembers fondly. 'I was so pampered I wasn't even allowed in the kitchen. So it was fun to pretend I was domesticated!'

The experience of making *Ijaazat*, as well the finished film, are both things that Rekha looks back on with reverence and affection. 'There's no "art" or "commercial" in cinema,' she posits. 'Just fake film and real film. *Ijaazat* was real. In fact, it's not just a film for me, it's a fond memory, like *Khubsoorat* and *Ghar* (1978). When you make something that's close to your soul, it's relished forever.'

ॐ

In the original story, Mahendra tries to get an emotional response out of Sudha in the waiting room by repeatedly asking her if she misses him or thinks about him, and eventually the story ends with her telling him that he should come visit her and her husband and children at their farmhouse so that he can witness how contented she is and stop having thoughts of a reconciliation. Gulzar omitted all of this, even though he liked that that's the note Sudha left on, because he didn't want his characters behaving in what he saw as stereotypically melodramatic ways. He sees them as good people stuck in an impossible situation. 'All three are trying to do what they think is the right thing; to not hurt the other,' he explains. 'Mahendra tries to forget Maya and move on, even though he knows that she must be in turmoil. Similarly, Sudha discovers how intense the relationship was and feels so deeply for Maya's pain that she removes herself from the equation. On the other end is Maya, who refers to Sudha as "didi" and doesn't want to create strife between the couple, though sometimes she can't help herself.'

Some scenes that explored these nuances wound up on the cutting room floor. Gulzar recalls one of them: 'There was a scene which took place when Maya comes to look after Mahendra after his heart attack. One day he's having one of his many cups of tea when Maya walks in wearing a sari. He looks at her and asks why she's dressed like that. She says she wanted to look more grown up so she put on one of Sudha's saris. He tells her very firmly, 'Don't touch her clothes. Take this off right now and put it back. You want

a sari, I'll buy it for you. Don't touch any of her things.'
This was a pivotal scene because it showed what a strange
predicament he was in; that he truly loves Maya but also
has immense respect and regard for Sudha, so much so that
he's telling off the woman he loves! I don't really remember
why this scene had to be cut, possibly because of duration.
But what a poignant situation for all three of them, trying
to extricate each other, salvage each other, but to no avail;
like a ball of thread, you pull one end, then another, then
another, but only get more and more entangled in the
process. And for a while, in their own ways, they imagine
that somehow they can go on as is.'

He goes on: 'Human beings are such an interesting
species. What an amazing creation of God; or maybe
His mischief! He made us and then left us to flounder,
watching what we'll do. And in the whole history of
humanity, no two humans or their realities have been
identical; each and every one has lived an individual life
and set of circumstances. That's the beauty of the human
race. And that's the beauty of writing, too, because in
writing you're exploring all the possibilities of human life
and there's no formula to it. You find something new with
every character.'

chapter seven

Do Humsaaye The

The Music Men

☙

'Gulzar had a special creative kinship with R.D. Burman and their relationship did not have the slightest trace of formality. As long as the versatile music composer was alive and when Gulzar was free to choose, he would always opt for R.D. Burman.'[32]

The professional and personal association between the director and the late music maker known affectionately as Pancham is, needless to say, the stuff of Bollywood legend. In an industry where creative partnerships often slide into artistic decay or personal acrimony, their pairing was as enduring as it was endearing and the fruit borne by the Gulzar-Pancham team remained sublimely sweet from

---

32 Chatterjee, *Echoes & Eloquences*, p. 77.

beginning to end. The two had struck up a friendship during the time when Gulzar first starting working with the senior Burman under Bimal Roy and they resolved early on to work together whenever Gulzar turned director. Over the course of more than thirty years of friendship that followed, the two produced some of the most memorable musical soundtracks ever heard in Hindi cinema. Of the fifteen feature films that Gulzar directed from 1971 to 1990, nine were scored by R.D. Burman, including such classics as *Parichay*, *Aandhi*, *Kinara* and *Khushboo*. As a team, and as friends, they had what the filmmaker has referred to as their special 'tuning': 'Working with him was such a pleasure. We understood each other's expressions and taste.'[33]

Artistically speaking, theirs was a symbiotic relationship; neither of the two men ever really found it necessary to elaborate to the other what was required – it was just understood. Even though Pancham's fluency was in Bangla and English, according to Gulzar, and he didn't know much Hindi beyond what he read and sang for his songs, 'he knew that whatever *ulta-seedha* (weird material) I brought to him was unique.' Their closeness and fruitful professional relationship used to irk some other filmmakers who would complain to the composer that he didn't give them the kind of music that he gave for Gulzar's films. The director recalls: 'He once said to Nasir Hussain, "You

---

33 Gulzar and Kabir, *In the Company of a Poet*, p. 150.

bring me music cassettes and tell me, 'make me something that sounds like this.' Gulzar just takes whatever I make for him." Another time he told me that while composing, he sees the singer in his mind; he knows how they'll sing the song, the kind of vocal flourishes they'll use, like didi [Lata Mangeshkar] for instance. "But there are certain kinds of songs that while composing them I'll see your *thobda* (face) in my head and I put them aside because I tell myself [that] only he will take these, nobody will else will want them." So, somewhere he knew exactly what my choice was; I never had to explain it.'

The fact that they were such good friends also led to an enviable comfort and camaraderie in their working relationship that often resulted in happy accidents, such as the one that occurred when they were working on the music for *Kinara*. Unlike most other directors, Gulzar wasn't content to simply hand over a music assignment and wait for the composer to deliver the tunes; he involved himself in the entire process and in the case of Pancham: 'It was a great help to be around him during the whole exercise of composing, rehearsing and recording. For example, when he would compose the interludes, I used to sit with him; not to make suggestions but to learn from him because his music would inspire my images.' In this instance, the composer was recording the song '*Ek hi khwaab*', sung by guitarist-cum-singer Bhupinder and to be picturized on Dharmendra in the film. Gulzar had originally written it for a film called *Mera*

Yaar Pocketmaar, which was ultimately never completed, but it fit in well with the requirements of a particular sequence in *Kinara* so he had Pancham set it to a new tune. Gulzar was present for the recording and describes what occurred: 'Right near the end of the take, there was a disturbance in the track. Some wire got pulled or something, resulting in an odd noise, a glitch, when we played it back. Pancham said we'll have to record another take but I said it wasn't necessary, I'd manage it in the picturization. He looked at me askance and said, "*Dekh lo,* don't blame me later!" But somehow, musically, I liked the sound.' When Gulzar shot the song, he created a situation in which Aarti (Hema Malini) and Chandan (Dharmendra) are playing cards and the latter pulls out a Joker from his hand, kissing it. 'The noise became the sound of Chandan kissing the card!' Gulzar remembers amusedly. 'Later, when Pancham watched the scene with me during a trial screening, he turned to me and slapped me on the shoulder. "*Saala!*" he exclaimed. "*Wah!*" We lived for those lovely moments.'

This deep understanding of how songs visually translate to the screen served the Gulzar-Pancham team well on many occasions, from the frenetic exuberance of '*Saare ke saare*' in *Parichay* to the deceptively simple but cinematically and musically complex composition of '*Ghar jayegi*' in *Khushboo* to the off-beat rhythm structure and haunting visualization of '*Tere bina zindagi se koi*' in *Aandhi.* The last, along with its spoken interludes, became so iconic that the soundtrack was released with the dialogue included; the heartbreak in Suchitra Sen's immortal line – '*Nau baras lambi thi na?*' ([The night] lasted nine years, didn't it?) – carried forward into an unbearably beautiful melancholy with Pancham's aching musical strains. Gulzar readily acknowledges the role that the composer played in the creation of these indelible moments: 'Pancham understood the medium of cinema very well and we were both concerned about the impact [the songs] would ultimately have in the film. Creatively, if you get to live such moments, what more do you want? Whether the film runs for twenty weeks or ten days, that is not the real enjoyment. Your creative satisfaction lies in this: the process of creation itself; how you created it, how thoughts and ideas multiplied, how each person made their contribution. And his contribution cannot be put into words adequately.'

Of course, R.D. Burman, too, expressed his admiration for Gulzar and his awe at the poet's way with the lyrical word on more than a few occasions, even as he admitted that he often struggled to grasp the nuances of his collaborator's expression. 'Gulzar is amazing. I have to be careful composing for him. I would sometimes need a day or two to understand the significance and beauty of his lyrics,' he stated in an interview in 1992,[34] possibly echoing

---

34 Aniruddha Bhattacharjee and Balaji Vittal, *R.D. Burman: The Man, the Music*, Noida: HarperCollins Publishers India, 2011, p. 298.

the sentiments of many others who, over the years, had been at once bewildered and bewitched by the distinctly modernist flavour of Gulzar's poetry. Although he himself had been weaned on the traditional and the classic, Gulzar, as a poet and lyricist, trod a path that was anything but conventional – constantly experimenting with syntax, idea structure and phonetics in such a way that it evoked powerfully oneiric imagery in which the abstract and the representational became engaged in a seamless pas de deux. This aspect comes across even when he describes the writing process: 'When I write a poem, it is like painting. I describe the dawn or sunset as if I were recreating it with a brush, though I am using a pen to write the words.'[35] One of the earliest instances of this use of tangible abstraction in his oeuvre was in a song from the cult favourite *Khamoshi*. The film contained superlative songs composed by Hemant Kumar, including '*Tum pukar lo*' and '*Woh shaam kuch ajeeb thi*', both of which became big hits. But it was a third song that became the subject of much scrutiny and debate, in particular the opening line: '*Humne dekhi hai un aankhon ki mehekti khushboo*' (I have seen the aroma of those eloquent eyes). 'I was heavily criticized and even teased for writing this kind of poetry,' Gulzar recalls. 'But thanks to Hemant Kumar, who was a celebrated singer of Tagore's songs and

---

35 Alter, *Fantasies of a Bollywood Love Thief*, p. 81.

could easily relate to this kind of imagery, the song worked.'[36] Needless to say, in time both critics and audiences would come to not only appreciate this quality of the poet's work but to eagerly expect and await it as well. By the time that he wrote '*Musafir hoon yaaro*' for *Parichay*, there was nothing but applause for the evocative verse in which phases of the day became old friends enticing the wanderer away from his meandering travels to come reminisce with them instead: '*Din ne haath thaam kar idher bitha liya/raat ne ishaaray se udher bula liya*' (The day took my hand and sat me here/the night beckoned me and called me there).

For the soundtrack of *Ijaazat*, both Pancham and Gulzar pulled out all the stops, creating a four-song tour de force that not only showcased their individual and collective best but also ended up becoming half of that year's one-two musical punch, along with their acclaimed private album *Dil Padosi Hai*. As it happened, both records featured the formidable vocal talents of the legendary Asha Bhosle. Long-time collaborators on countless song classics through the 1960s and 1970s – '*Aaja aaja main hoon pyaar tera*', '*Dum maaro dum*', '*Piya tu ab to aaja*', '*Chura liya hai tumne*', to name a few – Bhosle and Pancham had also tied the knot in 1980, becoming a partnership in every sense of the word. The singer said about their relationship: 'Music was the basic foundation of our marriage. We could listen

---

36 Gulzar, *100 Lyrics*, p. 25.

to Bismillah Khan, the Beatles, Shirley Bassey ... and so many more for hours and hours. Pancham would emerge from his shower in a lungi-kurta at 9.30 a.m. and till 3 p.m. we'd be humming together to the albums of John Coltrane, Earth, Wind and Fire, Sergio Mendes, Santana, the Rolling Stones, Blood Sweat and Tears, Chick Corea, Osibisa ... oh so many. Our taste in music was eclectic, and that was our everlasting bond.'[37]

Originally, the script of *Ijaazat* had space for only three songs and the main footage had been shot accordingly. The effervescent '*Chhoti si kahani se*', which ended up as the title song, was never meant to be in the film and was the result of another of those happy accidents that Gulzar and Pancham's partnership engendered. The director had been mulling over what to shoot for the opening title sequence. 'I had the visuals of the title sequence in mind,' he says. 'I knew the story involved a rainy night at a railway station so I wanted to make a visual symphony of rain, but that was all I had thought about it.' In the interim, he and Pancham met up for one of their casual evenings in the latter's music room.

'It wasn't a sitting; we were just relaxing and listening to some LP,' Gulzar recalls. 'There was a musical phrase in

---

37 Sharon Fernandes, 'Asha Bhosle: The bad girl of playback singing', *Dailyo*, 28 August 2017, https://www.dailyo.in/arts/asha-bhosle-lata-mangeshkar-rd-burman-playback-singing-film-industry/story/1/19116.html, accessed on 29 November 2018.

it which kept repeating itself. You'd hear the phrase a few times, it would go on to something else, but then it would come back again and repeat itself. It fascinated [Pancham].' The composer asked Gulzar to improvise a few lines that would fit this musical phrase. The director came up with '*Chhoti si kahaani se, baarishon ke paani se*' (with a little story, with the monsoon rains). Pancham used that, then started adding to the repetitive phrase: '*Na jaane kyun dil bhar gaya, na jaane kyun aankh bhar gayi*' (Don't know why my heart became heavy, don't know why my eyes filled with tears).

'That part had nothing to do with the original phrase on the LP; that was all Pancham. He said that this is turning out really good, let's complete it. He pulled out the harmonium and started playing.' As the two went on adding to it, Gulzar started wondering whether there could be a situation for the song in *Ijaazat*. 'Pancham said, "Can you fit it somewhere? It won't fit in any other film." I said everything is done, complete already, but I'll see.' Gulzar thought about it but knew there was no situation for it in the story. 'Then it struck me – we could play it over the titles! Obviously, we couldn't use the whole song because the titles weren't that long but at least it would be there, and we could have the complete song included on the soundtrack LP.'

For a song that was added as an afterthought, '*Chhoti si kahani se*' blends into the narrative quite effortlessly. Although, from a musical perspective, its vibrant mood and upbeat rhythm form a sharp contrast to the other more tonally contemplative songs of the film, a connection is established through the lyrics and visuals. As the first notes unfold, we are introduced, through cameraman Ashok Mehta's dazzling cinematography, to a dreamlike landscape of sumptuous green hills and cloud-cloaked valleys. A train snakes through the setting and bare tree branches look on, glistening with the remnants of a downpour that plays an ongoing game of hide-and-seek with the terrain. It's not hard to discern that, whether by design or felicity, the song is a subtextual twin to '*Katra katra milti hai*', which occurs later on in the film. The powerful word-imagery of the droplets in the latter song find a visual and lyrical echo in the water motif here while the haunting beauty of a rain-soaked scenery forms the backdrop to both, neatly and subtly underlining the past-present link that is so central to the story. And it is Pancham's brilliant orchestration, particularly the use of two primary accordions producing a restless, undulating refrain, that contributes to the dual motifs of cascading water and the rhythmical turning of the wheels of a train. Gulzar was more than pleased with the result: 'The song gives the feeling of rain, and the way rainwater dances and pours off the roof of a train. In that way it's a total dance number! And I picturized it accordingly. The late Ashok Mehta gave me that visual symphony of rain that I had in mind already for the visuals and Pancham gave me the perfect music to go with it.'

The story behind the making of 'Mera kuch saaman'
is arguably as famous as the song itself now and, in fact,
Pancham had had a similar reaction earlier when Gulzar
had asked him to compose 'Ek hi khwaab' for Kinara. The
composer thought that he had been handed a scene to read
and praised its poeticism. 'It's not a scene,' Gulzar told him.
'It's a song.' Pancham was aghast. How was he supposed
to put this 'free-verse nonsense' to music? The scenario
repeated itself when the director presented 'Mera kuch
saaman' to be composed. 'The story of Pancham's reaction
when I gave him the song has become legend, of course,'
Gulzar says fondly. 'He read it and then shoved the notebook
away. "Tomorrow you'll bring me an issue of the Times of
India and expect me to compose that too. You are the limit!"
He'd say to me, "You don't have any sense of metre, and how
can I make a mukhda (opening chorus) when there are no
rhyming lines?" ' Asha Bhosle was present at the sitting and
listened quietly to the exchange. As the clearly frustrated
Pancham tinkered aimlessly with his harmonium, the singer
nonchalantly began to hum the phrase 'lauta do' (return it
to me) from the song. 'Almost like a child reciting a nursery
rhyme,' as she'd later describe it. Pancham's ears pricked up
and he asked her to hum it again. Bhosle did so. That was all
the inspiration the composer needed. His hands went flying
on the harmonium and he completed the entire tune in
that very sitting. 'At the end of the day, he trusted me,' says
Gulzar. 'So in this instance, even though it exasperated him,

what a song he made out of it – constructing the whole thing out of just one simple phrasing.'

Gulzar's oft-overlooked skills as a visual filmmaker come to the fore in the picturization of the song. There are no audacious camera moves or showy cuts but a simplicity and sparseness that echo the sorrowful nostalgia of both the words and the situation. Maya wanders through her empty home, lit only by the hazy sunlight streaming through the windows. As she sings, a wistful smile plays on her lips even as her eyes brim with tears that she will not shed. Interspersed with these images are flashbacks of her past with Mahendra, yet another way in which Gulzar asserts the spectre of the past in the present – it is always there but you can never return to it. Maya is dressed all in white, like so many ethereal women of film, but her comportment does not denote the saintliness of Nutan singing '*Jogan ban ayi hun*', nor the sexualized languor of Zeenat Aman chanting '*Satyam shivam sundaram*'. It's as if she's an apparition in her own ghost story, forever doomed to live in a house of memories from which there is no escape.

But it's the mix of the abstract into the tangible in the lyrics, underlined by the intricate restraint of the score, that further lends the song its stirring, pensive beauty. The *saaman* (baggage) that Maya seeks the return of is not material but memory. A few rain-soaked monsoon days, a night wrapped in the delicate folds of a letter whose flame must be extinguished, the whispers of falling leaves from a tremulous bough that she had worn as ornaments – again, Gulzar weaves enchantments by giving abstract ideas a magical physicality. As Ulhas Bapat's wondrous interludes on the santoor create a reverie-like ambiance, Asha Bhosle's soulful voice embodies Maya's yearning as she sings of the 116 moonlit nights (*ek-sau solha chaand ki raatein*) she left behind with Mahendra. 'It's not the number which is important,' Gulzar posits. 'It's important that somebody kept the count of the moonlit nights which they spent together.'[38]

Initially, even the lyrics of '*Katra katra milti hai*' appeared to irk Pancham. '*Yeh kya katra katra laga rakha hai. Aese koi gaana banta hai?*' (What is this drop-by-drop nonsense. How can I make a song out of that?), he asked in annoyance, as he felt that *katra* wasn't a musical word.[39] As always, he soon seemed to have made peace with what he was given and became engrossed in coming up with a tune. But something was up. 'When he was composing "*Katra katra*", he wouldn't let me sit in on the sessions,' remembers Gulzar, 'which was unprecedented in our relationship. He kept putting me off,

---

38 Kanupriya, 'Mera Kuchh Saamaan (Ijaazat)', *Gulzar 101*, 16 September 2011.

39 Ziya Us Salam, 'Not worthless after all…', *The Hindu*, 19 April 2014, https://www.thehindu.com/todays-paper/tp-features/tp-sundaymagazine/not-worthless-after-all/article5929524.ece, accessed on 29 November 2018.

making excuses like "Oh, we'll do it tomorrow." He had something in mind and he was doing this on purpose.' When it finally came time to record the song, Pancham did something completely unexpected. The orchestra started, the rhythm came in and the vocal began. 'He recorded the first track and had Ashaji sing only part of the first line. Then he recorded the second track and had her sing the second half of the line, and so on. I was confused and asked what was going on but he motioned me to be quiet, "Just listen." Then when he played it back, the lines were overlapping; the beginning of one playing over the end of the previous one. He looked at me and said, "Now let's see you picturize this!" This was his challenge to me!'

Gulzar's solution was simple yet ingenious: wherever the lines overlapped, he dissolved from one shot of Rekha lip-synching to the next; thus, the 'melting' effect of the visual aptly duplicated that of the sound (once again, Pancham was stumped when he saw the result). And the landscape of Kudremukh provided the perfect backdrop to a song about a woman's seemingly willing acceptance of the love that she is compelled to share with another: '*Paa ke bhi tumhari aarzu ho/ shayad aise zindagi haseen hai/ aarzu mein behne do/ pyaasi hun main pyaasi rehne do*' (Even after attaining you I want you/ perhaps this is why life is beautiful/ let me stay adrift in my desire/ let my thirst not be quenched). Desire that is half-thwarted but half-fulfilled has an allure of its own, Sudha seemed to be saying. Elsewhere, in the line

'*girte girte baahon mein bachi main/sapnay pe paon pad gaya tha*'
(I nearly fell into your embrace/I had tripped on a dream),
one could discern traces of an earlier Gulzar classic from
Khushboo: '*Do nainon mein aansoo bhare hain/nindiya kaise
samaaye*' (my eyes are filled with tears/they have no room
for sleep). In the two songs, both dreams and sleep take
on physical dimensions and become hindrances in love's
way. It is these hidden but implied dualities in the lyrics of
'*Katra katra milti hai*' that give it an underlying melancholia,
despite the vibrantly romantic overtones of its melody
and rhythm.

The lurking ennui that is only alluded to in '*Katra katra
milti hai*' comes to the fore in '*Khaali haath shaam ayi hai*',
a song that is as beautiful as it is overwhelming in its sense
of disconsolate resignation. Elsewhere, Gulzar wrote of the
forlorn enchantment that defines the time we call evening:

Raat aur din kitne khubsoorat do waqt hain
aur kitne khubsoorat do lafz
In dono lafzon ke beech mein ek waqfa aata hai
jisay shaam ka waqt kehte hain
Yeh woh waqt hai jisay na raat apnaati hai
na din apne saath lekar jaata hai
Iss chhode hue, ya chhutay hue
lawaaris waqt se
shaayr aksar koi na koi lamha chun leta hai
aur see leta hai apne shairon mein

Lekin koi koi shaam bhi aisi baanj hoti hai
ke koi lamha de kar nahi jaati

(Night and day are such gorgeous times
    and two such gorgeous words
There is a pause between the two words,
    called evening
And this is a time that neither the night will take
    ownership of,
nor the day carry alongside
From this left-behind time,
this slipped-through-fingers, orphaned time,
poets pick a moment and stitch it into their poetry
But then again, some evenings are so barren,
they leave without granting a single moment)

Pancham's choice of Pilu as the base raga for '*Khaali
haath*' is a masterstroke; its familiar sombre strains make the
song reminiscent of Burman Senior's Pilu-based Bengali
number '*Ami chinnu eka baashor jaagaye*', which he adapted
into a Hindi version for *Meri Surat Teri Aankhen* (1963) in
the form of '*Tere bin soone nain hamare*'. The song opens
with heavy classical notes on the veena, which then most
improbably segue into a synthesized flourish that is repeated
and elaborated upon by a santoor before being joined
by a combination of guitar and tabla. At this point, Asha
Bhosle leads in with her velvet vocals, the dejection in her

enunciation locked into a duet with Pt. Ronu Majumdar's haunting work on the flute for the rest of the song. This ensemble of flute, guitar, santoor and tabla, with a subtle reso mixed in, settles into a comfortable melancholic groove. But what would a Pancham composition be without a flash of the unexpected? So, in the interlude for the second verse, he interjects a passage on the sitar that provides a sudden exteriority in its out-of-place-ness, almost like a third voice that speaks up to drop a note of hope into the proceedings. But it is not to be: Sudha's despair is too far gone and runs too deep for such false notes of feigned bravado; the flute quickly overtakes the sitar and returns the song to its mournful state, which is then sustained to the end. Pancham was especially pleased with how the song shaped up. 'It sounds like a Madan Mohan song, doesn't it?' he exclaimed happily to his director.[40]

As ever, Gulzar's poetry speaks volumes with its simplicity of form but complexity of thought in 'Khaali haath'. The empty-handed evening in the title takes on a human form, a haunting ghostly presence that returns again and again to remind Sudha of the state of hopelessness that her life has slid into. As she sings of tears that her eyes refuse to surrender to – 'aaj bhi na aaye aansoo/ aaj bhi na bheege naina' (on this night, too, tears stayed away/ on this night, too, my eyes did not well up) – Sudha's defiant words sound feeble.

---

40 Razdan, 'Gulzar on Ijaazat?'

Her resignation means that the night, whose starkness seeks relief in Sudha confronting her feelings, will be thwarted. In the second verse, there is a subtle but astounding play on words that beautifully reveals the complex and ambiguous duality of Sudha's own frame of mind: '*Raat ki siyahi koi aaye to mitaye na/Aaj na mitayi tau yeh kal bhi laut aayegi*' (Won't someone come and wipe away the blackness of this night/ lest the black night returns again tomorrow).

At first glance, and as translated, the words appear to be pleading for someone to come and take away the darkness and the pain of the night, for otherwise it will come around over and over again. But the insertion of the tricky word *na* offers a far darker, devastating suggestion: Sudha isn't calling for someone to wipe away the darkness, but to let it be. For if the darkness remains, she is at least assured that the night will return; and it returning with its bitter familiarity is better than it not returning at all. The impossibility of her situation, that her life and her being are lost both with and without Mahendra's fractured love, is thus captured powerfully and poetically.

Visually, the song is, of course, a companion piece to '*Mera kuch saaman*'. Where the latter showed Maya as the captive spirit haunting her surroundings and unable to move on, Sudha takes on that role here as she similarly wanders her empty home, the blackness of the evening outside threatening to engulf her inside. Again, the intensity of the scenario is created through thoughtful camera movement, timely edits and a superb, high-contrast lighting design that emphasizes its function as a mood piece. Gulzar credits his cinematographer for the picturization's lyricism: 'While picturizing the song, Ashok Mehta set up a beautiful shot with a red streak of light flooding in and reflecting on the floor. I had the entire imagery of the scene in my mind. But Ashok took a cup and saucer, and placed it in the circle of light. Then he poured a little tea in the saucer and tilted the cup in the saucer. The empty cup created such a powerful imagery of emptiness that it struck a chord. As a director, I may get credit for the scene but it was actually Ashok Mehta's contribution.'[41]

By any account, the soundtrack of *Ijaazat* was a highlight for both Gulzar and R.D. Burman in careers already overflowing with musical masterpieces. And, indeed, it was both a bestseller and a critical success in its year of release. But where Gulzar and Asha Bhosle were rewarded for their contribution to the songs – the former receiving both the Filmfare and the National Award for Best Lyricist, and the latter the National Award for Best Female Playback Singer (for *'Mera kuch saaman'*) – Pancham was overlooked entirely. This was just the latest slight in what had always been a contentious relationship between the composer and the milieu of movie awards, particularly the Filmfare. In the 1960s, he had not received a single nomination for Best

---

41 Razdan, 'Gulzar on Ijaazat?'

Music Direction; not for the ground-breaking music of *Teesri Manzil* (1966) or the chart-topper *Padosan* (1968). The 1970s – in which his was far and away the name that loomed larger than any other in the realm of film music – he wasn't bestowed with the award even once and his songs for *Amar Prem* (1972) and *Aandhi*, arguably two of his greatest works, weren't even nominated. It seemed that the powers that be in the film world, while eager to profit off of Pancham's boundless talent, were also jealous and resentful of his success. They wanted to 'put him in his place', as it were, by repeatedly ignoring the superiority of his work and instead showering awards on music that was glaringly inferior to his. By the time they got around to recognizing him, with his wins for *Sanam Teri Kasam* (1982) and *Masoom* in 1983 and 1984 respectively, it was too little too late. Pancham's star was already on the decline.

The 1980s had seen Bollywood descending rapidly into an artistic nadir, with a crude, action-oriented sensibility replacing the elegant romanticism of the previous decades. In this environment, there was scarcely any room for the melodious film music being created by the likes of R.D. Burman and he could only watch helplessly as his stock quickly plummeted. From being the most in-demand and successful film composer of the 1970s, he became almost a persona non grata. Purveyors of cinematic din and drudgery had no use for his otherworldly sophistication. At the age of fifty-four, barely seven years after *Ijaazat*, he died of a heart attack. It felt like tragicomic irony, then, that his last big film score, for Vidhu Vinod Chopra's *1942: A Love Story* (1994), became a massive success and he was awarded the Filmfare trophy for Best Music Direction posthumously, with Filmfare also instituting an award for new emerging musical talent in his name. Cold comfort, indeed, for a man who had felt abandoned and let down by so many whose careers he had been instrumental in establishing.

In 2008, Pancham aficionado Brahmanand S. Singh made the acclaimed biographical documentary *Pancham Unmixed: Mujhe Chalte Jaana Hai*. In the intervening years after his death, Pancham and his music had become more popular than ever with rereleases and remixes flooding a seemingly insatiable market. Gulzar appeared in the film in his trademark white pajama-kurta and fondly recounted memories of his relationship with Pancham. At one juncture, his voice faltered, heavy with feeling, as he spoke of the moments they had shared, moments that were 'full, brimming with emotions.' The film ends with Gulzar reciting the following poem:

Yaad hai baarishon ke din, Pancham
Yaad hai jab pahaadi ke neeche vaadee mein
dhundh se jhaank kar nikalti hui
rail ki patariyaan guzarti theen
Dhundh mein aise lag rahe the hum
jaise do pauday paas baithe hon

Hum bahut der tak wahan baithe
us musafir ka zikr karte rahe
jisko aana tha pichhli shab, lekin
uski aamad ka waqt talta raha
Der tak patariyon pe baithe hue
train ka intezar karte rahe
Train aayi, na uska waqt hua
aur tum yoon hi do kadam chal kar
dhundh par paon rakh ke chal bhi diye
Main akela hoon dhundh mein, Pancham.

(Remember those rainy days, Pancham?
Remember how the railway tracks
used to play hide-and-seek through the mist
that cloaked the valley below the hill?
In the mist we resembled
two plants huddled close together.
We sat there for so long
talking about the traveller
who was to have arrived the night before
but whose time never came.
We sat by the tracks for an eternity
waiting for the train.
It never arrived, its time came and went.
And, just like that, you took a few steps
ascended the mist
and wandered away.
I'm still alone in the mist, Pancham.)

chapter eight

Katra Katra Milti Hai

Aftermath

ભ

The box-office for Gulzar's films has rarely been stratospheric and, upon release in January 1987, *Ijaazat* was no exception. But it was a big critical success, the music was a massive seller and, in the decades since its release, the film has also found a steadily growing audience of newer and younger fans in addition to older loyalists. Most are drawn first to the music, whose popularity has not dwindled in its thirty years, and then go on to discover the equally rewarding joys of the narrative itself. The film is often found playing on any number of cable movie channels and its home video sales have been consistently strong. In some ways, it was also one of the last hurrahs of the middle cinema movement, a genre whose space grew smaller in the 1980s and then smaller still in the 1990s when Hindi films started aggressively wooing the NRI (non-resident Indian) audiences with glitzy urban love stories rather than tales of human interest. Stalwarts of the movement like Hrishikesh Mukherjee and Basu Chatterjee slowly retreated to the peripheries of the film industry; their gentle, lyrical sensibility finding few takers in this new era of big-budget glamour.

As for Gulzar, he made only three more films after *Ijaazat*, hanging up his director's hat for good with the 1999 political drama *Hu Tu Tu*. He intuitively knew that neither his style of filmmaking nor his concerns as a storyteller gelled with the newer tastes within and outside the industry. Changing mores also meant that he could no longer expect the kind of control over the finished product that he had once commanded. 'Writers often imagine they can fill the chasm between the written word and the final film,' he muses. 'But once you direct a film, you realize that this can never entirely happen. People who market the film can delete scenes or re-edit them — basically change the work.'[42] This kind of lack of control is, however, not a given in one's literary endeavours and that was the deciding factor for Gulzar: 'A book does not suffer the same fate [as a film]. What you imagine can be brought alive through words and the words on the page are largely unaltered. I had a lot of books in my head and still do. I have a limited number of years ahead of me, so I had to draw the line

---

42 Gulzar and Kabir, *In the Company of a Poet*, p. 98.

somewhere. That's why I decided to stop making films and return to literature from where I began.'[43] Saibal Chatterjee sees another angle when it comes to pondering why, in the wake of the director's bowing out, the 'Gulzar school' didn't flower among new filmmakers, considering how many he has worked with and been something of a mentor to: 'The reason probably is that Gulzar is really one of a kind; a man whose creative output cannot be imitated by the less gifted. His films, like his poetry, have sprung from a sensibility that is innately unique. It is a sensibility that isn't consciously cultivated. It is purely germane to his personality.'[44]

This, however, does not mean that Gulzar has said farewell to the industry and will never look back. If anything, since his retirement as a director he has, as a personality, become one of Bollywood's biggest stars, solely on the strength of being the industry's most celebrated – and decorated – lyricist. He has won successive new generations of admirers with monster hits like '*Chappa chappa charkha chale*', '*Chhaiyya chhaiyya*', '*Kajrare*', '*Beedi*' and countless others. The word-imagery and unique linguistic construction that were criticized once upon a time are now so beloved, and instantly recognizable, that many younger poets try, fruitlessly, to imitate them. But Gulzar himself is wary of becoming formulaic and tries to make sure

---

43 Gulzar and Kabir, *In the Company of a Poet*, p. 99.
44 Chatterjee, *Echoes & Eloquences*, p. 4.

that his writing stays fresh and ever-evolving: 'You need to consciously break away from a set pattern of thinking. I usually get bored with a subject or a writing style and there's nothing more tedious than repeating oneself. That's how I try to avoid formula.'[45]

Clearly, he must be doing something right for, to date, he has won a staggering twenty Filmfare awards, more than any other individual, across four different categories: screenplay, dialogue, direction and lyrics. In the early days, his nerves often kept him from going to award ceremonies but now, in his words, 'I am quite shameless [and] collect every award that I am given.'[46] He did not, however, make it to what is arguably the biggest award ceremony in the world of cinema: the Oscars. When A.R. Rahman won the 2008 Academy Award for Best Song – *'Jai ho'* from *Slumdog Millionaire* (2008) – Gulzar, as lyricist, was his co-winner but was unable to go because, he claims, he did not have a black jacket! The song also went on to win him a Grammy. Back home, he had already received the prestigious Sahitya Akademi Award in 2002 and India's third-highest civilian award, the Padma Bhushan, two years after that. In 2014, when he was awarded the Indian film industry's most distinguished accolade, the Dadasaheb Phalke Award, he thought of his father: 'I thought if he were here he could

---

45 Gulzar and Kabir, *In the Company of a Poet*, p. 101.
46 Ibid., p. 67.

see his son is not worthless after all.'[47] The Nobel is the only major prize that eludes him. So far.

Other than A.R. Rahman, Gulzar's most frequent collaborator in recent years has been composer-filmmaker Vishal Bhardwaj; in their personal and professional relationship, one senses traces of the Gulzar–Pancham duo (hardly surprising, considering that Bhardwaj is an avowed Pancham devotee). Starting with the mellifluous score for Gulzar's penultimate directorial effort *Maachis* in 1996, the two have worked together on numerous occasions, producing bestselling soundtracks such as *Satya* (1998), *Omkara* (2006), *Kaminey* (2009), *Ishqiya* (2010) and *Haider* (2014). Gulzar greatly admires Bhardwaj for his ability to be brutally self-critical and stated at a retrospective of his films in Ladakh in 2013 that he considers the composer-director his son: 'I say it because I like him. That is why he is my son. Many a time I have said this that I see an extension in him – *uski wajah se jitni umar thhi usse zyada jee raha hun* (because of him I'm living longer than I would have otherwise). He is *mere apne* for me and amongst the closest to me.' For his part, Bhardwaj, too, calls Gulzar not only a mentor but also a father to him and considers *Ijaazat* the ultimate romantic film. In an interview for Indian cinema website The Big Indian Picture, the filmmaker states: 'I want to make a film like *Ijaazat*. I think that's one of the

---

47 Salam, 'Not worthless after all...'

most romantic films ever on the Indian film screen. And
'*Mera kuch saaman*' is one of the best romantic songs that
Indian films have seen.'

A popular invitee at every manner of film and literary
festival around the world, Gulzar has paced his activities in
recent years; although, as he enters his eighty-fourth year,
his literary output is still impressively prolific. He is usually
found writing away furiously at a crowded work desk in
his Pali Hill home (christened Boskyana after his daughter).
Precious souvenirs and artwork dot the adjoining sitting
area where he entertains formal guests and journalists, with
whom he continues to be a popular interviewee. He and his
wife, Rakhee, have lived separately since the '70s but remain
close friends; she is often over at the house, chatting, cooking
and singing '*Mujhse pehli si mohabbat meri mehboob na maang*'
at her husband's urging. Gulzar is a doting grandfather to
his grandson Samay and takes great parental pride in his
daughter Meghna's (Bosky) success as a filmmaker. Meghna
credits her father for teaching her the value of simplicity:
'It reflects in his persona, his life choices and his work.' She
also finds inspiration in his writing and his philosophy as
a filmmaker. 'I love the brevity of his writing, the delicacy
of his expression and thought. The one thing he tells me is,
"Keep the purity of the language and please promise me
your son will too." [As a filmmaker] what I learnt from
him is that even though making money is important, it is

equally important for your film to leave a lasting impression on the audience.'[48]

Of course, many times films leave lasting impressions on their makers, too, which is certainly the case with Gulzar. About the process, he says: 'Sometimes a film doesn't simply follow a straight line when you're making it – you know, pre-production, production, release, then you're done with it – it goes beyond that, because the filmmaker is a part of it and it is a part of him. You're not outside of it and it is not outside of you. For example, when I was making *Koshish*, Sanjeev, Jaya (Bachchan) and I all learned sign language. To me, it wasn't a film for the sake of making a film; I felt responsible for whatever I was portraying in it. *Koshish* was over forty years ago but I'm still involved with Aarushi, the organization that helps to rehabilitate those children with hearing disabilities. So, whatever you say in your film, or you write in your books, somewhere there is a commitment to it. And that commitment is larger than the film or the book. It stays with you. And *Ijaazat* ... *Ijaazat*, too, has stayed with me.'

---

48 Veenu Singh, 'Meghna Gulzar respects parents for raising her together, separately', *Hindustan Times,* 28 February 2016, https://www.hindustantimes.com/brunch/meghna-gulzar-respects-parents-for-raising-her-together-separately/story-eB2WDjgq4wir46EaNH3X5H.html, accessed on 29 November 2018.

Bibliography

⚬

Alter, Stephen. 2007. *Fantasies of a Bollywood Love Thief: Inside the World of Indian Moviemaking*. New Delhi: Harper Collins Publishers.

Anirban. 3 July 2013. 'Of failed marriages, waiting rooms, and cups of tea'. *Milkmiracle*, https://milkmiracle.net/2013/07/03/of-failed-marriages-waiting-rooms-and-cups-of-tea/, accessed on 29 November 2018.

Bhattacharjee, Anirudha, and Balaji Vittal. 2011. *R.D. Burman: The Man, the Music*. Noida: HarperCollins Publishers India.

Bose, Mihir. 2008. *Bollywood: A History*. New Delhi: Lotus Collection, Roli Books.

Chatterjee, Saibal. 2007. *Echoes & Eloquences: The Life and Cinema of Gulzar*. New Delhi: Rupa & Co.

Chawla, Ankita. 3 April 2017. 'Picture the song: "Mera Kuch Samaan" is about all that you leave behind in love'. *Scroll*, https://scroll.in/reel/833525/picture-the-song-mera-kuch-samaan-is-about-all-that-you-leave-behind-in-love, accessed on 29 November 2018.

Fernandes, Sharon. 28 August 2017. 'Asha Bhosle: The bad girl of playback singing'. *Dailyo*, https://www.dailyo.in/arts/asha-bhosle-lata-mangeshkar-rd-burman-playback-singing-film-industry/story/1/19116.html, accessed on 29 November 2018.

Gulzar. 2009. *100 Lyrics*. New Delhi: Penguin Viking.

Gulzar, and Nasreen M. Kabir. 2012. *In the Company of a Poet*. New Delhi: Rainlight.

Gulzar. 2013. *Pluto*. New Delhi: HarperCollins Publishers India.

Jain, Madhu. 2009. *The Kapoors: The First Family of Indian Cinema*. New Delhi: Penguin.

Jha, Pavan. 2 August 2017. 'Gulzar kii...Chhoti Si Kahani Si'. *Apnaarchive*, https://apnaarchive.wordpress.com/2017/08/02/gulzar-kii-chhoti-si-kahani-si/, accessed on 29 November 2018.

Kanupriya. 16 September 2011. 'Mera Kuchh Saamaan (Ijaazat)'. *Gulzar 101*.

Pearson, Carol, and Katherine Pope. 1976. *Who Am I This Time?: Female Portraits in British and American Literature*. New York: McGraw-Hill.

Power, Chris. 24 May 2013. 'A brief survey of the short story part 49: Guy de Maupassant'. *The Guardian*, https://www.theguardian.com/books/booksblog/2013/may/24/survey-short-story-guy-de-maupassant, accessed on 29 November 2018.

Rabin, Nathan. 16 July 2014. 'I'm sorry for coining the phrase Manic Pixie Dream Girl'. *Salon*, https://www.salon.com/2014/07/15/im_sorry_for_coining_the_phrase_manic_pixie_dream_girl/, accessed on 29 November 2018.

Razdan, Shalini. 19 June 2006. 'Gulzar on Ijaazat?', newsgroups.derkeiler

Salam, Ziya Us. 19 April 2014. 'Not worthless after all...', *The Hindu*, https://www.thehindu.com/todays-paper/tp-features/tp-sundaymagazine/not-worthless-after-all/article5929524.ece, accessed on 29 November 2018.

Saari, Anil. 2011. *Indian Cinema: The Faces Behind the Masks*. New Delhi: Oxford University Press.

Singh, Veenu. 28 February 2016. 'Meghna Gulzar respects parents for raising her together, separately'. *Hindustan Times,* https://www.hindustantimes.com/brunch/meghna-gulzar-respects-parents-for-raising-her-together-separately/story-eB2WDjgq4wir46EaNH3X5H.html, accessed on 29 November 2018.

Somaaya, Bhawana. 2013. *Talking Cinema: Conversations with Actors and Film-Makers*. Noida: HarperCollins Publishers India.

Zacharek, Stephanie. 2010. 'Nonfiction: My Year of Flops: the A.V. Club Presents One Man's Journey Deep into the Heart of Cinematic Failure. By Nathan Rabin.' *The New York Times Book Review*, 13.

Acknowledgements

CR

There are many people without whose support this book would never have seen the light of day. I thank them all profusely.

First and foremost, Gulzar saheb himself, for his generosity, eloquence and insights, for welcoming me into his home and for letting me into his memories.

Naseeruddin Shah for indulging me and my questions without complaint, and Ratna Pathak Shah for that fabulous vegetarian meal.

Anuradha Patel for taking out time to speak to me at length over the phone, despite the mini-crisis she was contending with at the time.

My childhood idol Rekha, in whose presence I became a tongue-tied twelve-year-old again, for her warmth and candour. I also want to thank her and her secretary, Farzana, for giving me a lift to the taxi stand on that rainy Mumbai evening.

Bina Sarkar and Rafeeq Ellias for their wonderful hospitality in Mumbai, and for plying me with delicious food at every opportunity.

My editor, Shantanu Ray Chaudhri, for his encouragement and infinite patience.

Danish Hussain for arranging things in Mumbai and for always picking the best films to watch at the cinema.

Faiza Sultan Khan for instigating this whole thing in the first place.

Martand Khosla and Sapna Desai for putting me up – and putting up with me – in Delhi and giving me the room with the biggest TV.

Anirudha Bhattacharjee for his memes and songs sent over WhatsApp that always provided a chuckle, and for his sympathy when I repeatedly got writer's block – 'It's okay, yaar, I'm stuck too.'

My little sister-from-another-mister, Kyla Pasha, for her help with translations and for generally being brilliant.

My coterie of friends and family in Lahore and elsewhere – too many to name – who continue to inspire me with their boundless love and fierce loyalty. You know who you are, you awesome creatures.

My gorgeous mother-in-law, Farida Ghias, who is always a pillar of support whenever life gets too crazy.

ACKNOWLEDGEMENTS

My husband, Waqas, whose words of motivation – '*Jaani, ab khatam kar bhi lo*' – provided just the right kind of kick in the pants.

And finally, my kids Anya and Faiz, who make me laugh every single day, while also astonishing and humbling me with their wisdom.